Roots Of The Spirit

Supernatural Breakthrough For Nine Key Areas Of Life.

DONNA FRIEND

WESTBOW
PRESS®
A DIVISION OF THOMAS NELSON
& ZONDERVAN

WestBow Press books may be ordered through booksellers or by contacting:

WestBow Press
A Division of Thomas Nelson & Zondervan
1663 Liberty Drive
Bloomington, IN 47403
www.westbowpress.com
1 (866) 928-1240

Scripture quotations taken from the Amplified® Bible (AMP), Copyright © 2015 by The Lockman Foundation Used by permission. www.Lockman.org

Scripture quotations marked (NLT) are taken from the Holy Bible, New Living Translation, copyright ©1996, 2004, 2015 by Tyndale House Foundation. Used by permission of Tyndale House Publishers, a Division of Tyndale House Ministries, Carol Stream, Illinois 60188. All rights reserved.

ISBN: 978-1-9736-8601-9 (sc)
ISBN: 978-1-9736-8600-2 (e)

Print information available on the last page.

WestBow Press rev. date: 03/03/2020

Contents

Foreword

We are all familiar with the saying, "There is nothing new under the sun". Donna Friend has produced a work which can say, "There's plenty new under this Son".

Come; discover the many insights produced from years of deep relationship with God which Donna has skillfully applied to her successful counseling practice.

Dive into a deeper understanding of yourself and how easily you can be set free to access greater liberty and intimacy with God.

Benefit from the author's insights into Scripture, her prophetic gifting, and the prayers for release and commitment found throughout <u>Roots of the Spirit</u>.

Having put into practice many of the recommended strategies in my own life, I can testify to having experienced spiritual break-through on a new level.

<u>Roots of the Spirit</u> is a Kingdom work for today's seriously committed Christian who desires to acquire a greater knowledge of the workings of the Holy Spirit as never before

In Hosea 4:6 we read, "My people are destroyed for lack of knowledge". Tap into <u>Roots of the Spirit</u> yourself and find out what you are missing. See if you can agree with me that Donna Friend can truly say:

> "My heart is overflowing
> With a good theme; I
> Recite my composition
> Concerning the King.
> My tongue is the pen
> Of a ready writer."
> Ps: 45:1

Sincerely,
Karen Oliver

Introduction

John 8:32 (NLT)
32 and you will know the truth, and the truth will set you free."

This book is a compilation of the little insights (truths) that I have learned from the Lord over the past few years while counseling people to a place of freedom in Christ. The words on these pages are designed to assist you in interceding for yourself and others from a posture of revelation. We are so blessed to serve a God who wants to reveal the hidden secrets of this world and to inspire us with fresh revelation from His Word. As we spend time with Him and apply the revelation we receive to our lives, we see a spiritual breakthrough in places that we never imagined could be possible. It's exciting to pray things through with God and see change happen for ourselves and those around us. We can also impact what is happening globally with our prayers. God wants us to partner with Him in this process. It's up to us to accept or reject His invitation.

These writings were birthed from my own experiences as well as the experiences of those around me. I have entitled this book Roots of the Spirit because the issues we deal with in our lives have roots that usually go down deep into the center of our being. These roots are mainly spiritual or emotional and they are causing outward physical or mental symptoms. My desire is that with each chapter we will reach the main root or taproot for each subject covered.

A taproot is the main root of a primary root system; it grows vertically downward. Most dicotyledonous plants, such as dandelions, produce taproots. The edible taproots of carrots and beets are designed for food storage. The taproot allows for other roots to offshoot from it as well. If you have ever tried to pull a dandelion out of the ground, you know how long, deep, and strong the taproot can be. If you aren't successful at getting the entire taproot removed, the dandelion will eventually grow back. This is a perfect analogy of what happens in our lives. If you don't destroy or pull a spiritual/emotional issue out at the root, it will have permission to grow again.

Within these chapters, you will find various subjects each of which I believe God has blessed me with some insight. There are ways to be pro-active in destroying a stronghold which is causing problems for you or a family member or friend. Sometimes one of these strategies will hit the core (taproot) and destroy the root that is feeding the entire issue. You may find these techniques and approaches quite helpful but they may not necessarily be the total answer to your problem. Sometimes the root is removed; yet, some behaviors may need to be changed by renewing your mind with God's Word and changing some habits. My prayer is that some of these insights will be nothing short of miraculous in your healing!

My findings reveal the importance of not only praying over the taproot to bring about its destruction but also to decree and declare a positive, opposite declaration over the situation or issue. By utilizing this method we are agreeing with heaven and destroying negative roots and replacing them with positive fruits.

Galatians 5:22-23 Amplified Bible (AMP)
22 But the fruit of the Spirit [the result of His presence within us] is love [unselfish concern for others], joy, [inner] peace, patience [not the ability to wait, but how we act while waiting], kindness, goodness, faithfulness, 23 gentleness, self-control. Against such things, there is no law.

James 3:17 Amplified Bible (AMP)
17 But the wisdom from above is first pure [morally and spiritually undefiled], then peace-loving [courteous, considerate], gentle, reasonable [and willing to listen], full of compassion and good fruits. It is unwavering, without [self-righteous] hypocrisy [and self-serving guile].

You will see as you move through these pages that the subjects are quite varied. There is not one congruent theme to these chapters other than my findings on successful ways to get to the heart of each matter. I hope you find this book interesting reading filled with breakthroughs for healing with a few aha moments thrown in for good measure.

Chapter one

Music

Psalm 59:17
To You, O [God] my strength, I will sing praises; For God
is my stronghold [my refuge, my protector, my high tower],
the God who shows me [steadfast] lovingkindness.

Music is a powerful tool created by God. It's important to begin this chapter by defining music. dictionary.com defines it as:

an art of sound in time that expresses ideas and emotions in significant forms through the elements of rhythm, melody, harmony, and color.

the tones or sounds employed, occurring in a single line (melody) or multiple lines (harmony), and sounded or to be sounded by one or more voices or instruments, or both.

Music is important to us as human beings. It can encourage us and boost our mood when we are feeling depressed. Certain songs remind us of our younger years and what was happening in our lives during those times. A once forgotten tune can bring back a flood of memories and emotions in a most powerful way. Music can rock us to the core when we hear a song that reminds us of a sorrowful time or the loss of a loved one. Music is ultimately for the worship of the Triune God. God also created music to touch our very souls and bring healing through a release of emotions. Music can bring us to a place of feeling revived if it is coming from the Kingdom of heaven. But what happens to this beautiful, sacred gift from our Creator when Satan perverts it? Let's take a look at what Scripture tells us about his nature:

Isaiah 14:11-15 Amplified Bible (AMP)
11 'Your pomp and magnificence have been brought down to Sheol,
Along with the music of your harps;
The maggots [which prey on the dead] are
spread out under you [as a bed]
And worms are your covering [Babylonian rulers].'
12 "How you have fallen from heaven,
O [a]star of the morning [light-bringer], son of the dawn!
You have been cut down to the ground,
You who have weakened the nations [king of Babylon]!
13 "But you said in your heart,
'I will ascend to heaven;
I will raise my throne above the stars of God;
I will sit on the mount of assembly
In the remote parts of the north.
14 'I will ascend above the heights of the clouds;
I will make myself like the Most High.'
15 "But [in fact] you will be brought down to Sheol,
To the remote recesses of the pit (the region of the dead).

Most biblical scholars agree that this Scripture has a two-fold meaning. It refers to the king of Babylon and also directly to Satan himself. Let's see what Jesus said which confirms this reference to Satan when He quoted the prophet, Isaiah:

Luke 10:17-19 Amplified Bible (AMP)
17 The seventy returned with joy, saying, "Lord, even the demons are
subject to us in Your name." 18 He said to them, "I watched Satan
fall from heaven like [a flash of] lightning. 19 Listen carefully: I have
given you authority [that you now possess] to tread on [a]serpents
and scorpions, and [the ability to exercise authority] over all the
power of the enemy (Satan); and nothing will [in any way] harm you.

Everything the enemy touches he perverts. We see in the above Scriptures that Satan is full of pride, he is a liar, and he is not creative. He can not create. God creates. The enemy of our souls takes the beautiful things that God has created and twists them in order to use them against us. Music is no different. Many speculate that Satan was in charge of worship in heaven. When pride overtook him and he decided that he wanted to exalt himself above our Most Holy God, there was a battle in heaven and he and a third of the angels that revolted with him were kicked out of heaven.

Jude 6 Amplified Bible (AMP)
6 And angels who did not keep their own designated place
of power, but abandoned their proper dwelling place,
[these] He has kept in eternal chains under [the thick gloom
of utter] darkness for the judgment of the great day,

Regardless of whether Satan was in charge of worship in heaven or not, he was privy to knowledge about music into which we may not have the full insight. With the knowledge we do have regarding music, we must realize that songs can be a help or a hindrance to our lives.

There are many variables that can make a musical piece helpful or harmful to your soul realm and physical body.

It has been a long-held belief that certain types of music are demonic, but we are in a time where we believe that God is redeeming music for Himself. What the enemy has used in music to harm us, God is redeeming. This means that He can use rock, rap, hip-hop, country, folk, classical, etc., to encourage and edify the body of Christ. As we are being set free from religion, we as the Body of Christ are no longer vilifying any type of music that we don't personally like. Today we see all different styles of praise and worship music that honors Jesus.

Music is such a beautiful gift from God. We see in the Old Testament how David's skillful playing on the harp could cause Saul to be at peace.

1 Samuel 16:14-16 Amplified Bible (AMP)
14 Now the Spirit of the Lord departed from Saul, and an
evil spirit from the Lord tormented and terrified him. 15
Saul's servants said to him, "Behold, an evil spirit from God is
tormenting you. 16 Let our lord now command your servants
who are here before you to find a man who plays skillfully
on the harp; and when the evil spirit from God is on you, he
shall play the harp with his hand, and you will be well."

Do you remember when you got saved? Did you suddenly hear music in a different way? I speak with many new believers who can, upon salvation, listen to a secular radio station and recognize the lyrics from a favorite love song. That song is now directed to their love and devotion of their Lord and Savior instead of toward a human lover. It seems to happen automatically within them as their first love has now become Jesus. I believe that this is another way God redeems secular music for us.

The other spiritual awakening I have discovered is that many new believers begin to become aware of is how unholy many of the lyrics contained in the secular music they used to or still are listening to really is. Many Christians are actually surprised as to how blind they were to what they used to enjoy on the radio. In my own experience, as well as that of many others, it seems we are quite appalled at the things we sang and came into agreement with as we were entertained by these songs.

Proverbs 13:3 Amplified Bible (AMP)
3 The one who guards his mouth [thinking before he
speaks] protects his life; The one who opens his lips wide
[and chatters without thinking] comes to ruin.

Psalm 109:17
He also loved cursing, and it came [back] to him; He
did not delight in blessing, so it was far from him.

James 3:10
Out of the same mouth come both blessing and cursing.
These things, my brothers, should not be this way [for we
have a moral obligation to speak in a manner that reflects
our fear of God and profound respect for His precepts].

What we speak or sing, we are speaking and singing over ourselves. We know that we possess the power to bless and curse by what comes out of our mouth. We can create with what we speak or sing. We create our future, we create our own mindsets as we hear what we are saying or singing with our own ears. Many of us have sung hundreds, even thousands of songs that come into agreement with what the enemy wants for our lives. There is a large portion of secular music that is focused on rebellion, pride, selfishness, sex, pain, suicide, etc. We must become aware of anything with which we come into agreement.

We also need to be aware of which emotions surface as we hear old songs. This will give us a clear indication of how much music has affected us in our past and will continue to affect us in our present and future.

I want to share a story with you. I have a dear friend who suffered the loss of a child as well as the loss of her marriage. Her childhood and teenage years were laced with lots of rejection and rebellion. Every time she went shopping it seemed as though the songs which were playing from the past were so upsetting that sometimes she would have to leave her shopping cart and just get out of the building. This was greatly troubling to her. She understood her authority in Christ and knew that there must be a way to stop this cycle. As we prayed, the Lord instructed us to pray and renounce those songs and lyrics. She was completely set free! Now she can go into any place where those old songs are playing and they have zero effect on her!

More than a decade ago I had another acquaintance who was struggling with wanting a divorce. She would complain weekly at our Bible study that she just wasn't happy and was feeling like she had missed out on something better. Nothing was helping her pull out of this funk. Finally, one week, as we were praying for her, someone in our prayer group sensed in their spirit to ask her what type of music she was listening to. She stated that she had been listening to an oldies station that played the music from the years when she was a teenager. As we further questioned her about how she was feeling during those years, she immediately began to get the connection between the music and how she was currently feeling about her husband. Those songs were taking her back in a soulish, unhealthy way to the times when she was young and free from the responsibilities of caring for her children and home. She reminisced about how good it was to be free from paying bills and all the challenges being married can bring. She could even pinpoint that those feelings of discontent began at about the same time that she began listening to the oldies station. Those songs conjured up the old feelings in her soul and her physical body. It was taking her back to a time when there was no responsibility. Suddenly she felt trapped in her marriage as she came back into agreement through the power of the music of how life used to be. We prayed this prayer:

Dear Lord,

Please forgive me for knowing and unknowingly coming into agreement with unhealthy, unholy music. Forgive me for singing and professing those destructive, self-centered, lyrics over myself. I now renounce and break all agreements I made with all unholy music from my past and present in the Name of Jesus. I revoke its rights over my life, my marriage, and my children's lives in Jesus' Name. I plead the Blood of Jesus over my mind (conscious, unconscious, and subconscious) and over my emotions and my physical body in Jesus' Name. I command any unholy ties to be cut and disintegrated in Jesus' Name. I ask you, Jesus, to consecrate me when it comes to music. Holy Spirit, I ask you to give me an inner witness if I am coming into agreement with music in the future that is not honoring to Your Name. Redeem music for me in Jesus' Name. Amen.

I have multiple success stories on the heels of these examples. One woman kept feeling pulled back into having affairs. She loved God and was heartbroken over this propensity inside of herself. We also found for her that music was the open door to initiating the destructive thoughts that those relationships were better than being monogamous in her marriage. As we cut through the lies and broke the ties to the music that would pull her back, she saw a great breakthrough! If she heard those particular songs playing anywhere she traveled, they no longer had any effect on her emotions.

I also had my own personal breakthrough and release. I experienced that same heartache in the grocery store after my husband died. It seemed that oftentimes they were playing songs that would bring back a flood of memories and I also would find it difficult to finish shopping. I would pray and get through it but it wasn't easy. One day driving home after a particularly difficult shopping trip, I sensed the Lord encouraging me to do the same prayer work with myself. I prayed over myself utilizing the same basic prayer above. While in the middle of the prayer I also was taken back to a time in my teens when I was lying on the floor of my bedroom. I was singing a song to myself and God showed me how impactful that one particular song was in opening the door to rebellion in my own life. I broke agreement with all of the songs but especially prayed over the one song that God highlighted to me. I felt a physical release in my mind and I no longer experience any old emotional attachments to the songs of my yesteryear. It is so freeing!

Psalm 68:1-3 Amplified Bible (AMP)
To the Chief Musician. A Psalm of David. A Song.
68 Let God arise, and His enemies be scattered; Let those
who hate Him flee before Him. 2 As smoke is driven away,
so drive them away; As wax melts before the fire, So let the
wicked and guilty perish before [the presence of] God.
3 But let the righteous be glad; let them be in good spirits before God,
Yes, let them rejoice with delight.

I don't think that there is anyone reading this book that has escaped the negative effects of music. I encourage everyone to pray the prayer written above and to profess the positive declaration below. You have everything to gain and absolutely nothing to lose by doing so even if you don't believe you were affected.

I decree and declare that according to 2 Corinthians 7:1 that my old sin nature and the music that accompanied that time of my life no longer have a hold on me. I am cleansed from everything that contaminates my body and spirit, and what I choose to listen to sets me apart for God's purposes in my life. I confess this by faith in Jesus' Name. Amen.

2 Corinthians 7:1 Amplified Bible (AMP)
Paul Reveals His Heart
7 Therefore, since we have these [great and wonderful] promises,
beloved, let us cleanse ourselves from everything that contaminates
body and spirit, completing holiness [living a consecrated
life—a life set apart for God's purpose] in the fear of God.

CHAPTER 2

Nature

Isaiah 6:3 New Living Translation (NLT)
3 They were calling out to each other,
"Holy, holy, holy is the Lord of Heaven's Armies!
The whole earth is filled with His glory!"

The older people get, the more they seem to appreciate nature. I am wondering if it's because we seem so much more self-focused when we are adolescents and even into the decade of our twenties and beyond than we are later in life. As we begin to have our own children, we get to experience things through their eyes. It's so wonderful to watch a child experience the ocean for the first time or watch them explore the coldness and beauty of snow as their eyes widen with delight. I have also noticed that, after people get saved, many seem to be more appreciative of nature. Perhaps this is the Holy Spirit enjoying His own creation but this time they are experiencing His delight because He lives on the inside of them!

As my relationship has deepened in Christ, I believe God speaks to me more through His greenery. For example, when He was building my faith, He used my much-loved miniature lime tree to teach me spiritual truths. I had that tree for years and grew it from a tiny sapling. I was wondering if I would ever see a lime produced on its beautiful, green foliage. He began to nudge me to speak over the tree to "be fruitful and multiply in Jesus' Name." As I began to speak life over the tree, it finally began to flower and then to produce the most adorable, little limes! This lesson was a reminder of how powerful our words can be to bring life or death.

Proverbs 18:21 Amplified Bible (AMP)
21 Death and life are in the power of the tongue,
And those who love it and indulge it will eat its fruit
and bear the consequences of their words.

From there He began to speak to me as I weeded my garden, reminding me that unconfessed sin is like weeds. It's important to keep my garden weeded regularly, otherwise, the weeds will choke out the fruit. If you have ever hoed a garden with aggressive weeds, you know that some roots go down deep and disturb the other plants. Our lives are like that. If we don't expose and destroy those deep roots of unforgiveness and resentment, we minimize our own beautiful, spiritual harvest. Let's also not forget how we affect others as well:

Hebrews 12:15 Amplified Bible (AMP)
15 See to it that no one falls short of God's grace; that no root of
resentment springs up and causes trouble, and by it, many be defiled;

Over the years I have had many prophetic words given to me for myself as well as my family regarding nature on our property. God then began to utilize nature to speak to me prophetically about bigger issues such as the 2016 presidential election which was approaching that autumn. I had noticed that the leaves were not falling off of the trees in their usual, timely manner. I knew this had to be a prophetic sign and I questioned God about it. I felt as though He was saying that, as the leaves were delayed in falling off of the trees, so was He delaying the true reaping and sowing we could have received as a result of the unholy things we had allowed in this country. We instead received His beautiful grace economically as well as spiritually. Those of us who are prayer warriors know the countless believers who were on their knees for years imploring God for a much-needed turnaround. Hear my heart, this is not about any political affiliation. This is about God's grace and mercy on a country that didn't do anything to warrant it. Instead, the remnant prayed. I felt as though He was saying that those leaves represented His people in the U.S.A. and that we needed to remain connected to the "Tree" (so to speak) in order to usher in revival and the third great awakening which, I believe, we are now on the fringes of experiencing. It was an awesome prophetic sign! It brought much comfort to my soul.

The most recent root of the spirit, that God showed me, blew me away! I was in a prayer meeting with a group of believers who are like-minded and in much unity. We were worshipping and praying when a spirit of revelation descended into the room. What I heard next was so amazing to me that I feel like I am still trying to wrap my mind around it! I believe God was saying that there are keys to successfully praying for one's state that are found in nature within that state. If you live outside of the U.S.A, it would be for the region or district in which you live. Here in New Jersey, there are twenty-one counties. Each county is known for producing a certain type of fruit or vegetable, (i.e.certain counties are known for their blueberry or cranberry crop while others are known for their corn production.) Each of these different types of vegetation is harvested during different times of the year and each grows in different soils, conditions, etc. I believe that all of nature speaks in its own way. The Word says that all of nature reveals His glory. So why wouldn't His crops give us keys to advancing the Kingdom!

Romans 1:20Amplified Bible (AMP)
20 Forever since the creation of the world His invisible attributes,
His eternal power, and divine nature, have been clearly seen,
being understood through His workmanship [all His creation,
the wonderful things that He has made], so that they [who fail to
believe and trust in Him] are without excuse and without defense.

Romans 8:19Amplified Bible (AMP)
19 For [even the whole] creation [all nature] waits
eagerly for the children of God to be revealed.

I believe because He spoke everything into creation that creation speaks His hidden secrets back to us through their silent, yet highly visible attributes.

Psalm 19:1-2Amplified Bible (AMP)
The Works and the Word of God.
To the Chief Musician. A Psalm of David.
The heavens are telling of the glory of God;
And the expanse [of heaven] is declaring the work of His hands.
Day after day pours forth speech,
And night after night reveals knowledge.

Psalm 148 says that the whole of creation is invoked to praise the Lord. Genesis chapter one speaks of how God created plants and trees for us for food and I believe that He can cause them to reveal secrets of how we are to pray. If God allows a plant species to flourish in an area, (regardless of whether another people group brought it with them to that region or it originally grew there) then I believe it can bear a message. It can bear a message when it brings forth harvest and anything else the Lord chooses to reveal to us through that plant. It can give us insight into praying for that specific county or region.

Let's take blueberries for example. A blueberry bush is hearty and can withstand some harsh winter weather. They require much hydration and New Jersey has high water tables. Here in the northeast part of the U.S.A., they are typically harvested in late June through mid-July. Blues are known for their high antioxidants which fight many types of diseases. The branches that are pruned back produce the most blueberries. So how do we break that down spiritually? Say for example we live in southern New Jersey which has claimed to be "The blueberry capital of the world." Its population increases dramatically during the summer due to proximity to the Atlantic Ocean. It is also known for much human trafficking in prostitution and slave labor! I believe that we are called first to pray and then to take the territory for the Lord in the area in which we reside.

With the belief that God can speak keys to taking this territory through that beautiful blueberry bush, your prayer may look something like this:

God, I thank You for all power and authority to decree and declare Your goodness over South Jersey! We call forth the abundance of the rain of the Holy Spirit over this area to water souls in Jesus' Name. In John 15:2 your Word says that "Every branch in Me that does not bear fruit, He takes away; and every branch that continues to bear fruit, He [repeatedly] prunes, so that it will bear more fruit [even richer and finer fruit]." Lord, the potential for harvest in this area is great in June and July. We declare that the harvesters will be great in the region to demonstrate Your love to the unsaved and that the harvest this year will be abundant and plentiful! We ask for the strategy to eradicate the cancer of slavery in this area. Prepare our hearts during the offseason to be ready to assist those who need us when summer comes. Give us eyes to see and ears to hear what You are saying for this upcoming crop of people who are ripe for the picking and need Your everlasting love. Let us do great exploits for You releasing miracles, signs, and wonders. In Jesus' Name, amen.

Let's jump across the nation to the state of Idaho. How about that Idaho potato crop that is so famous? Did you know that they are grown from other cuts of an actual sprouted potato and not a seed? They grow so well due to the amount of rich minerals from volcanic ash in that area. The potatoes are ready when the top of the plant dies off and all the nutrients have been pushed into the potato. They require lots of water and Idaho is blessed to have lots of snowmelt runoff.

Prayer in this region may look something like this:

God your Word says in Proverbs 25:13 that "Like the cold of snow [brought from the mountains] in the time of harvest, so is a faithful messenger to those who send him; For he refreshes the life of his masters."We decree and declare a multiplication and duplication of believers through discipleship in this region. Let us die to ourselves as we disciple others. Holy Spirit, please provide through us the nutrients to enrich those coming up in the Kingdom in this next generation. May we have an unmatched ability to produce healthy growth in the body of Christ in this area and may they go out and impact the Kingdom wherever they go. In Jesus' name, Amen.

Recently I was in my car praising God and I felt like He shared that some earthquakes are actually the rocks crying out their praise to Him. He didn't cause the earthquake, so to speak, it's a spiritual law built into creation:

> **Luke 19:39-40 Amplified Bible (AMP)**
> **39 Some of the Pharisees from the crowd said to Him,
> "Teacher, rebuke Your disciples [for shouting these
> Messianic praises]." 40 Jesus replied, "I tell you, if these
> [people] keep silent, the stones will cry out [in praise]!"**

> **Matthew 27:50-51 Amplified Bible (AMP)**
> **50 And Jesus cried out again with a loud [agonized] voice and gave
> up His spirit [voluntarily, sovereignly dismissing and releasing His
> spirit from His body in submission to His Father's plan]. 51 And [at
> once] the veil [of the Holy of Holies] of the temple was [a]torn in two
> from top to bottom; the earth shook and the rocks were split apart.**

Have you ever listened to the chirp of a bird or the sound of a whale and think that it is speaking a message? Job 12:7-8 confirms this:

> **Job 12:7-8 Amplified Bible (AMP)**
> **7 "Now ask the animals, and let them teach you [that God does
> not deal with His creatures according to their character];
> And ask the birds of the air, and let them tell you; 8 Or speak to
> the earth [with its many forms of life], and it will teach you;
> And let the fish of the sea declare [this truth] to you.**

> **Psalm 50:10-11 Amplified Bible (AMP)**
> **10 "For every beast of the forest is Mine,
> And the cattle on a thousand hills.
> 11 "I know every bird of the mountains,
> And everything that moves in the field is [a]Mine.**

Scripture confirms repeatedly how nature speaks. We need to be spiritually in tune to what is being spoken. Nature will give us an inclination of what is happening and confirm prophetic words. They work together. This is a root of wisdom that was built into creation from the very beginning. Don't ignore this very valuable tool which is continually speaking, sometimes in a loud roar like a tsunami or earthquake, and sometimes in silence.

Dear Lord,

Please show me what Your Spirit wants to reveal to me through nature. May You, Holy Spirit, find all of my senses awakened to what You want to speak to me through your creation. In Jesus' Name, I pray, amen.

Declaration: I decree and declare that as God's people, we have full access to the wisdom and hidden keys in Your creation. We thank You, Lord, that even now You are unlocking the riches of Your works to us and we will steward them wisely through our prayers to destroy the works of the enemy and to bring many into the Kingdom of Heaven.

> ***Psalm 104:24 Amplified Bible (AMP)***
> ***24 O Lord, how many and varied are Your works!***
> ***In wisdom You have made them all;***
> ***The earth is full of Your riches and Your creatures.***

Chapter 3

Dementia/Alzheimers

Revelation 3:20 Amplified Bible (AMP)
20 Behold, I stand at the door [of the church] and continually
knock. If anyone hears My voice and opens the door, I will
come in and eat with him (restore him), and he with Me.

It may surprise you that I am writing about these two abnormalities. As of this writing, there are no known cures and it seems that more and more people are suffering from these diseases. I believe that dementia-like symptoms can come from the toxins in our environment such as processed foods, pesticides, genetically modified products, sugar, gluten, etc. The list can go on and on. Just like I believe that autism can be brought about by toxic vaccines. Can I go so far as to say that I have also seen unholy roots to dementia/Alzheimers and feel as though I have some answers based on my own experiences which I will share in this chapter.

As I looked at more research, I began to find multiple mature believers who suspected the same. In fact, a few doctors who are believers have written about these perceived roots of memory-type maladies. Their research has concluded that resentment, bitterness, unforgiveness, as well as issues such as low self-worth and self-hatred lend greatly to Alzheimers and dementia. You see, if we don't get a grip on the reality that our mind controls our body, we won't have the proper information to be healed. In fact, when we gain this understanding prior to symptoms of these diseases manifesting, we can take charge of our health. By the time the symptoms begin to present themselves, it can be much more difficult to get a person focused on being set free.

Let's dig a little deeper. Dementia is just an umbrella term that Alzheimers disease can fall under. A person who is unknowingly leading up to a stroke can present like a dementia patient. If a scan is not performed, no one may be aware of the impending stroke(s). We know that strokes are the result of the clogging of blood vessels. The brain then becomes blood deficient. According to one doctor who works scripturally with patients, he noted a trend in like characteristics of self-rejection, self-bitterness, and self-hatred. These people have not been able to tap into their identity in Christ. I blame most of this on the heavy religious atmosphere that has been in our country for at least one hundred years. I am only siteing one hundred years based on my knowledge of the family lines I have personally observed. If you watch and listen to what their relationship to God was, it appeared to be fear-based, not love-based. Many were punished to the degree that would be considered abuse today. This was done under the Scripture that reads, "Spare the rod and spoil the child." This opens the door for many walls of rejection, trauma, and mistrust toward others. There were also tons of rules and regulations put on these people and many were parented in judgment and criticism. Many had the view that God was angry and ready to smite them if they did anything wrong. When you put all of that together, it makes a cocktail for low self-worth and self-rejection as well as unforgiveness toward self and others (maybe even God).

Be grateful that you live during a time period when we are truly breaking out of all of that mess for God's purposes. There is so much more love being preached and demonstrated from God's people while still maintaining a healthy boundary and standards about sin. On the other hand, there are still major strides to be made regarding childhood abuse disguised as discipline.

I am taking a pause here to remind you that I am in no way a doctor and am citing what I have read and learned from others up to this point. I will now share two stories about people with whom I had the opportunity to interact in my own life and what I learned from their personal stories.

The first was a beautiful woman in my life who was of sound mind and body. She worked hard; her diet was pretty good and she appeared to be happy most of the time. The one key that was apparent most of her life was low self-worth. As early signs of dementia began to creep in, this became even more pronounced. She loved God and prayed daily. When I would try to speak to her about healing and a need to be set free, she seemed almost incapable of comprehending the concept. There was much religion and false humility steeped into her past due to her upbringing. There were soul wounds from feeling ignored and unimportant in her family as a child as well. As she began to share and release forgiveness toward these things as well as receive prayer for some traumatic events, she began to gain just enough mental territory back to begin to learn about her authority in Christ. She never understood it before because she felt worthless and powerless even though the Scriptures told her otherwise. There are many Scriptures telling us how we are to rule and reign in Christ Jesus. Here is my favorite:

Mark 16:16-18 Amplified Bible (AMP)
16 He who has believed [in Me] and has been baptized will be
saved [from the penalty of God's wrath and judgment], but he
who has not believed will be condemned. 17 These signs will
accompany those who have believed: in My name, they will cast
out demons, they will speak in new tongues; 18 they will pick
up serpents, and if they drink anything deadly, it will not hurt
them; they will lay hands on the sick, and they will get well."

As the lady was guided through prayers to take authority over her own mind and thoughts in the Name of Jesus, she was able to perform a few tasks better than she was able to when she didn't pray and take authority beforehand. After a short time period of seeing a small difference in her abilities when coupled with prayer, she finally admitted out loud with her own mouth that she believed that she had some authority. Within minutes of that verbal declaration, she vomited up a ball of mucous from the pit of her stomach which looked a bit like phlegm. She was surprised as she had just eaten; yet, this was the only item that was expelled from her digestive system. No food came up with that ball. This was not the first time I had seen this type of deliverance. I informed her that she had just been delivered from what I believed at the time to be an unholy tentacle of the religious spirit.

If that freaks you out, it shouldn't. Look at the deliverances in the Bible that Jesus performed when He walked the earth ministering to people. If you think you don't need deliverance as a believer, you must remember that when you get saved your spirit is regenerated. You still have a soul realm (heart, mind, emotions) and a physical body that is not regenerated. If the soul were regenerated, your whole being in totality would be perfect.

Let's get back to our patient. After vomiting that spiritual root up, she was then able to gain much territory back quickly. She was able to write again, read again, follow a recipe with assistance again, speak in fuller sentences and have much more clarity to her thoughts. It was miraculous. Sadly, within a few months, something unholy was able to reclaim the territory that was gained and she went backward quickly.

Do I look at that as defeat. For this lady, yes, but not for those of us who are still wanting to help others to be set free. One person's experience does not determine another person's outcome. In fact, one person's experience will assist in helping others just like it does in the medical field. I am hopeful and excited to see what other insights those working in the field of inner healing and deliverance will gain as they work with people who want to be healed. The most important concept to glean from this lady's life is to work with the Holy Spirit to get free from low self-worth and religion and learn to walk in your God-given authority.

The second person from whom I gleaned a spiritual insight was a male Alzheimers patient. I am not sure when the initial symptoms began to present themselves because I was not around him much. I am not even sure that his family closest to him could tell me either. Why? Because his lifetime demeanor was that of a quiet, mostly stubborn man with the joy of the Lord seeping out once in a while in between. Because he was fairly quiet, I believe it probably really began to take root much earlier than anyone realized. What is so interesting about this particular case is the level of resentment, bitterness, and unforgiveness this man walked in. I don't believe that he realized just how deeply all of it was rooted until the end of his life. He was not very forgiving toward people outside of his immediate family and held grudges that lasted a lifetime. As his disease progressed, it presented with: unexpected bouts of anger and rage as well as an inability to know what to do in emergency situations, driving down streets the wrong way, and eventually not remembering his age or current events, etc.

I am assuming if you are a believer, you know what God's Word says about unforgiveness, but just in case, here are a few references:

Matthew 18:21-22 American Standard Version (ASV)
21 Then came Peter and said to him, Lord, how oft shall
my brother sin against me, and I forgive him? until
seven times? 22 Jesus saith unto him, I say not unto thee,
Until seven times; but, until seventy times seven.

Matthew 6:14
For if you forgive others their trespasses [their reckless and
willful sins], your heavenly Father will also forgive you.

Matthew 6:15
But if you do not forgive others [nurturing your hurt and anger
with the result that it interferes with your relationship with
God], then your Father will not forgive your trespasses.

Back to this man's story. Not surprisingly, this man suffered a major heart attack one weekend. When the doctor shared the prognosis, it was not good. The doctor encouraged his wife to remove all life support because his heart was damaged beyond any possible repair. He noted that the man would not live more than a few hours if that. The wife determined that this was the highest act of love to let him go, especially since he was now becoming fearful and combative at home. The family had been praying that God would take him home before he no longer knew who he was or who anyone else was for that matter. It must be a very fearful state to live in during the late stages of Alzheimer's disease.

What happened next was incredible. By the next morning, the man was still alive and speaking. His wife began to sense through the Holy Spirit that her husband had some unforgiveness to work out before God could take him home for eternity. She began to bring up to him one by one, each person God laid on her heart to whom he needed to extend forgiveness and thereby release. This process took four days. The man had no food or water and only a sponge to his lips which often is done in these cases. Finally, on the fourth evening, his wife sensed that his list of grudges, resentments, and unforgiveness was finally taken care of with the Lord. She then felt released to begin to sing hymns to her husband. By the middle of the night, he passed away.

Am I going to say that if you die with unforgiveness in your heart, that you are not going to heaven? I wouldn't choose to make that judgment call. I am saying that God loves us so much that He knows how much religion and low self-worth, as well as this man's upbringing from childhood, had blocked him from knowing and walking in the pure love and identity of God. He was almost incapable in his present condition of rectifying his own wrongs. But God was faithful to make sure that his plate was clear before taking his last breath. What a loving God we serve!

If you have not gotten a clear understanding yet, I am saying that I believe that a major root of Alzheimers is unforgiveness. If you have resentment, bitterness, and unforgiveness in your heart, take care of it quickly with God. Ask the Holy Spirit to show you any forgotten record of wrongs that you are harboring against other people. He will be faithful to show you and will assist you in forgiving and releasing those who have hurt you.

If you are aware of any dementia/Alzheimers in your family line pray the following prayer:

Generational Forgiveness Prayer:

Dear heavenly Father,

I ask You to forgive me and I repent (turn away from) allowing generational iniquity into my life knowingly or unknowingly. I now renounce having participated in the sins of _____. (fill in the blank where you know that you are following in the same sins as those before you or don't want to receive as you age.) (Ask the Holy Spirit to bring to your mind anything that you have not thought of yourself.) I also choose to forgive myself and release myself.

I apply the Blood of Jesus and cut any cords that are attached to it and declare it won't go forward to future generations. I now stand in identificational repentance for anyone in my family, all the way back to Adam, and ask for forgiveness for them and I break the power (clap your hands) that those sins have over me and I put the cross of Christ between them and me and I again declare that it is broken in the Name of Jesus and it will not go forward to future generations.

I would also ask God to show you any current as well as old unforgiveness, resentment or bitterness that you are holding on to that you may not even be aware of. This process could take years if you tend to be slow to forgive. Every time you think about an old situation, ask yourself if you are holding onto anything that needs to be forgiven.

> ***Ephesians 4:25-27 Amplified Bible (AMP)***
> **25 Therefore, rejecting all falsehood [whether lying, defrauding, telling half-truths, spreading rumors, any such as these], speak truth each one with his neighbor, for we are all parts of one another [and we are all parts of the Body of Christ]. 26 Be angry [at sin—at immorality, at injustice, at ungodly behavior], yet do not sin; do not let your anger [cause you shame, nor allow it to] last until the sun goes down. 27 And do not give the devil an opportunity [to lead you into sin by holding a grudge, or nurturing anger, or harboring resentment, or cultivating bitterness].**

Verse 25 tells us how to stay out of bitterness. It says to speak the truth in love. You see, when we quickly speak the truth in love then we can forgive. Don't be a victim of your hurts. As you come into a place of releasing and forgiving everyone in your life, you will have much more mental clarity and peace.

That is just one of our responsibilities in keeping a sound mind as we grow older. We need to renew our minds by meditating on God's Word. We need to release ourselves from low self-worth and self-hatred. We also need to take care of our physical bodies, giving God the best living sacrifice available to be utilized for His glory as we step into our golden years.

Declaration: I decree and declare that I will present my body as a living sacrifice, holy and pleasing to God according to Romans 12:1. I know that my God will be faithful to continually reveal anything that could disturb my mental clarity and peace because of His great love and unfailing mercy.

> ***Romans 12:1 Amplified Bible (AMP)***
> **12 [a]Therefore I urge you, [b]brothers and sisters, by the mercies of God, to present your bodies [dedicating all of yourselves, set apart] as a living sacrifice, holy and well-pleasing to God, which is your rational (logical, intelligent) act of worship.**

Chapter 4

Obsessive-Compulsive Disorder

Matthew 23:4 Amplified Bible (AMP)
4 The scribes and Pharisees tie up [a]heavy loads [that are
hard to bear] and place them on men's shoulders, but they
themselves will not lift a finger [to make them lighter].

Another root stemming from the religious spirit is obsessive-compulsive disorder. Let's examine this in Scripture. If you know the Old Testament, you know that under the law if you committed a sin, you needed to perform a ceremony through sacrifice in order to be clean and in right standing with the Lord again. Let's look at some examples:

Leviticus 22:3
Say to them, 'Any one of your descendants throughout your
generations who approaches the holy things which the
Israelites dedicate to the Lord, while he is [ceremonially]
unclean, that person shall be cut off from My presence
and excluded from the sanctuary; I am the Lord.

Leviticus 4:4
He shall bring the bull to the doorway of the Tent of
Meeting before the Lord, and shall lay his hand on
the bull's head [transferring symbolically his guilt to
the sacrifice] and kill the bull before the Lord.

So we see here that a sacrifice had to be made in order to atone for sin. Under Christ, we have received His shed Blood once for all sin thereby nullifying the need for any other sacrifice. You may be saying at this point, "I know all of this and what does any of this have to do with the obsessive compulsive disorder?" Well, let's examine some of the traits of OCD that line up under religion. If we are involved in a religion instead of being in a relationship with God, we are required to go through certain routines and/or rituals each day that are repetitive. Maybe when we are a new convert, the rituals and routines are fresh and exciting. We do recognize that human beings can quickly fall into a pattern or rut. Patterns and rituals tend to give people a false sense of security. If your religion requires ritual in order to be acceptable, these rituals can quickly become a rote practice that has lost all meaning. We become robotic in our daily prayers and anything else required by a religion-inspired faith. Praise the Lord that we instead have a real relationship with two-way dialogue and a God who wants our time with Him to be fresh and different and exciting and full of dialogue and intimacy! This is a true relationship with the Father, Son and Holy Spirit and not religion.

A religious spirit will put you under bondage to rituals and routines. Let's see what Jesus said to those carrying religion and legalism in His day:

> *Luke 11:37-44 Amplified Bible (AMP)*
> *37 Now after Jesus had spoken, a Pharisee asked Him to have lunch with him. He went in [the Pharisee's home] and reclined at the table [without ceremonially washing His hands]. 38 The Pharisee noticed this and was surprised that Jesus did not first ceremonially wash before the meal. 39 But the Lord said to him, "Now you Pharisees clean the outside of the cup and plate [as required by tradition]; but inside you are full of greed and wickedness. 40 You foolish ones [acting without reflection or intelligence]! Did not He who made the outside make the inside also? 41 But give that which is within as charity [that is, acts of mercy and compassion, not as a public display, but as an expression of your faithfulness to God], and then indeed all things are clean for you. 42 "But woe (judgment is coming) to you Pharisees, because you [self-righteously] [a]tithe mint and [b]rue and every [little] garden herb [tending to all the minute details], and yet disregard and neglect justice and the love of God; but these are the things you should have done, without neglecting the others.*

The Pharisees had not only required the people to follow God's laws, but also they had added a bunch of their own. The original law was designed to show us that we were in need of a Savior and would not be able to be "good enough" to get to heaven on our own merits. The religious leaders heaped a bunch of other self-made laws and rules on the people as well and these became heavy burdens.

When you talk to a person with obsessive compulsive tendencies, you see lots of self-imposed rules and regulations that are now holding them in bondage just like the people were put under law and bondage by the leaders (Pharisees) during Jesus' time on the earth. People with OCD tendencies are driven by fear, and for many, a need for perfection. I have noticed the pattern that those suffering with OCD have a background involving religion or they have generational ties in the DNA to the religious spirit or legalism from their family within three to four generations prior to themselves. I don't find it funny that so many people lately refer to themselves as OCD in a joking manner. It's not something you want to proclaim over yourself. Those who are in bondage to OCD will tell you it's sheer torture.

Here are some of the characteristics that accompany this disorder:

Obsessions and compulsions can involve many different things, like an exaggerated need for order or cleanness, hoarding, intrusive thoughts about sex, religion, violence, and body parts.

Obsessive thoughts can include:

- Fear of germs or getting dirty
- Worries about getting hurt or others being hurt
- Need for things to be placed in an exact order
- Belief that certain numbers or colors are "good" or "bad"
- Constant awareness of blinking, breathing, or other body sensations
- Unfounded suspicion that a partner is unfaithful

This first group of listed symptoms are a torturesome way to exist. This is clearly not having a peaceful mindset and it's not from God. There is an interference to peace of mind and oftentimes it is rooted in a religious mindset. What if we grew up in a religious, legalistic home or church that focused more on works, perfection, judgment and our sin than they did on the relationship with our heavenly Father through Jesus? This is fertile ground for allowing religion to torture you in your mind and to affect your actions. Let's take a look at some of the compulsive habits that can accompany OCD:

Compulsive habits can include:

- Washing hands many times in a row even to the point of bleeding.
- Doing tasks in a specific order every time, or a certain "good" number of times
- Repetitive checking on a locked door, light switch, and other things
- Need to count things, like steps or bottles

- Putting items in an exact order, like cans with labels facing front
- Fear of touching doorknobs, using public toilets, or shaking hands

There are other causes of OCD behaviors such as trauma from an event or series of events in which you have fear and a need to control your environment. So what if you are saying, "I think this is me or this could possibly apply to me." First, ask yourself if you experience any of the following tendencies that indicate a religious spiritual influence:

- being judgmental
- self-righteousness
- religious pride
- criticism
- legalism
- perfectionism
- division
- error (doctrinal falsehood)
- unbelief
- doubt
- confusion
- argumentativeness
- false holiness
- salvation by works
- guilt
- lying
- condemnation
- fear of losing salvation
- fear of God (unhealthy, scared feeling)
- intolerance
- perversion

If you are struggling with any of these symptoms and also have any OCD tendencies, then let's take the necessary steps to break the power that the spirit of religion has over your life. The first step would be to pray the prayer to break the generational curse that may be plaguing your family line. Generational witchcraft or superstitions may also be a factor and are covered in the prayer below:

Dear Lord, please forgive me for walking in the generational sins and curses on my mother and father's side of the family. I also choose to forgive myself for walking in these curses. God, I ask you to forgive my ancestors all the way back to Adam and Eve on both sides of my family for opening the door to witchcraft and superstition, the religious/legalistic spirit which includes, being judgmental, self-righteousness, pridefulness, critical spirit, legalism, perfectionism and striving, causing division, doctrinal error, doubt and unbelief, confusion, being argumentative, possessing false holiness as well as false humility, trying to earn salvation by works, guilt, shame, condemnation, fear, lying, and intolerance. I now break the power that those sins and curses have over my life and I put the cross of Christ between me and them. I decree and declare that they will not go forward into future generations in the Name of Jesus. I cut every tie in the Name of Jesus. I also command any familiar spirits to leave now in Jesus' Name.

I wash my mindsets and bone marrow in the Blood of Jesus and I line my DNA up under the Father, Son, and Holy Spirit. I release your perfect love which casts out all fear and I put on the sound mind of Christ and ask you, Holy Spirit, to assist me in walking as Jesus walked in Your perfect love. Amen

I included washing our bone marrow in the above prayer because our marrow contains the deepest nature within us. Owlcation.com says, A bone marrow transplant may be needed when the patient's own marrow becomes damaged or fails to function properly. When donated stem cells enter the bone, they produce healthy and functioning stem cells as well as target unhealthy cells.

One problem with any type of transplant is that the recipient's body may attack and destroy the donated cells. This is why doctors look for donor cells that have membrane similarities to the patient's cells before they perform a transplant. The membrane is the outer layer of a cell. The body doesn't normally attack cells which it recognizes as "self". It distinguishes self from non-self by detecting the presence of membrane proteins.

The first time I felt led to plead the Blood of Jesus over someone's bone marrow came with someone that I felt was not wanting to give up perversion (which lines up with religion) at the core of their being. If you look at the Amplified version of Hebrews 4:12 you will see what God's word says about marrow.

Hebrews 4:12
**For the word of God is living and active and full of power
[making it operative, energizing, and effective]. It is sharper
than any two-edged sword, penetrating as far as the division of
the soul and spirit [the completeness of a person], and of both
joints and marrow [the deepest parts of our nature], exposing
and judging the very thoughts and intentions of the heart.**

Our marrow is the deepest part of our nature. God's Word and His Blood are the spiritual prescription to heal us in the depths of our nature. Let's also take a look at Proverbs:

Proverbs 3:7-8 Amplified Bible (AMP)
7 Do not be wise in your own eyes;
Fear the Lord [with reverent awe and obedience]
and turn [entirely] away from evil.
8 It will be health to your body [your marrow, your nerves,
your sinews, your muscles—all your inner parts] And
refreshment (physical well-being) to your bones.

The religious leaders of Jesus's day considered themselves wise. Their pride was exposed by Jesus in the Gospels.

Let's get back to the person whose bone marrow was being highlighted by the Lord. As God exposed the deepest part of this person's nature (their bone marrow) and the thoughts and intentions of their heart, He was able to cut through as this person surrendered that part of themselves to Jesus. As we prayed over their bone marrow, they felt an electric shock go through their bones. This person was a believer in Christ struggling with their sexual identity. Their marrow did not reject the stem cell transplant with the Blood of Jesus because they were already saved and their marrow already perceived His blood cells as "self" (a compatible transplant) because they (Jesus and the person) are one. How cool is that? This believer has been walking in victory over perversion since then. I love it when science and the Word of God confirm each other.

If we examine what Jesus told the Pharisees in John 5, we begin to see a few more significant keys to healing:

John 5:19-20 Amplified Bible (AMP)
19 So Jesus answered them by saying, "I assure you and most
solemnly say to you, the Son [a]can do nothing of Himself [of His
own accord], unless it is something He sees the Father doing; for
whatever things the Father does, the Son [in His turn] also does in
the same way. 20 For the Father dearly loves the Son and shows Him
everything that He Himself is doing; and the Father will show Him
greater works than these, so that you will be filled with wonder.

When Jesus walked the earth in human form, He only did what He saw the Father doing and/or speaking to Him. This freed Him up from being under anyone else's judgment or need for approval. He spent His ministry listening and walking in confidence that if

He heard and then obeyed, He could do miracles, signs, and wonders and fulfill the call on His life here on earth. Many with OCD tendencies are grabbing onto anything that they can to feel a sense of control in their personal world. Many tend to have a sense of worthlessness and to feel like a failure. A common trait is never feeling like they are getting enough accomplished within a day to feel good about themselves. Many feel as though they are not succeeding in life on the same timetable that everyone else around them appears to be.

OCD tendencies can begin to present themselves as a coping mechanism for control when they feel inadequate on a daily basis. Many fears have built up due to a lack of trust in themselves or God. Most people I have met with extreme OCD seem to have the thought that God does not favor them or they have a fear of loss of salvation. The only place left to look for approval when we don't approve of ourselves and we don't think that God approves of us is to look to others for our value and approval. Let's see what Jesus says about that further along in John 5 as He continues to address the Pharisees:

John 5:44 Amplified Bible (AMP)
44 How can you believe [in Me], when you [seek and] receive glory and approval from one another, and yet you do not seek the glory and approval which comes from the one and only God?

The Scribes and Pharisees sought glory and approval from man and not God. They kept adding more rules and regulations to the Scriptures and heaped heavy burdens on the people of God. I believe they did this not only for control, but also because they felt so unworthy within themselves and they were striving to find a way to be okay with themselves and feel loved and approved by God. They had a wrong view of their God.

Let me tell you that their example, in my experience, is how the majority of people suffering with OCD feel. It's so easy for someone who has never experienced these symptoms to just say something like, "Just trust God." Or "learn to love yourself." This is a stronghold in the mind that must be broken down. Unless someone is miraculously set free (I know that's possible with God), they will need to begin to tear down this stronghold one piece at a time.

Jesus had the right view. The Pharisees couldn't accept that. They had so much pride and fear. They were unwilling to release control of their environment to the Holy One of Israel. I believe Jesus gives us the key to breaking this part of the stronghold down by beginning to seek God's direction for our day and following what we believe He is saying about how to spend our time. This alleviates the daily striving to complete a million tasks which is unreasonable and stressful. We strive for the approval of others and to see if checked boxes on our list will fill the empty hole inside that says we are not good enough. When we begin to follow what the Father says to do for the day, we begin to have self-love and self-confidence because of who God is inside of us. We will need less and less approval from others. The only approval we will seek is that of our heavenly Father because we will be doing what we see and hear the Father saying.

If you feel as though you are not hearing clearly from God regarding your day, just go and do what you believe He is saying and trust that your heavenly Father will re-direct you if necessary. Recently I heard from a wise man in my life that it is easier for God to change the course or shift someone who is in motion than it is to redirect someone who is frozen and standing still waiting for God to speak.

Other helpful methods for tearing down the stronghold of OCD involve prayer, reading God's Word, spending time in His presence. This can include being still and listening for His voice or a leading in your spirit, resting and/or listening to soaking music. There are many anointed musicians who have godly soaking music to glean from. I will suggest a few that I choose to listen to on Youtube. Joshua Mills, Alberto and Kimberly Rivera, and Julie True are just a few examples. Learning to soak and rest is a big component in the tearing down of this stronghold. If you have a racing mind, you will understand that it is difficult to quiet yourself and rest in God's presence. If you need to start with just five or ten minutes per day, that is okay. It's better than what you were able to do when you were not connecting at all with God through anointed music. This is one of the practices that will help you begin to experience heaven here on earth.

If you experience a repetitive need to check on things such as a lock on a door, try giving some of the things you check repeatedly to another person whom you trust. This will begin to help you learn to depend on others. Sometimes this process is the beginning of trust. It can feel easier to trust a person you can actually see than surrendering things to God. You know that God wants to help you; yet you can't see Him and you aren't so sure you can trust Him with small, earthly things such as a lock on a door. A family member or roommate who is sympathetic to your OCD tendencies may be able to support you by taking some of the load off of your mind. If you know someone else is watching the lock on the front door or making sure the stove is turned off, would you be able to stop checking it yourself? It is the first small step in learning to lean on others for support and eventually trusting God. As you surrender control, you will think less and less about the lock on the door.

1 Peter 5:7 Amplified Bible (AMP)
7 casting all your cares [all your anxieties, all your worries, and all your concerns, once and for all] on Him, for He cares about you [with deepest affection, and watches over you very carefully].

One of my most beloved sections of the Bible is the book of First John. This book contains much insight into what a person suffering with OCD needs to meditate on in order to bring healing to their soul. Meditating on God's Word allows the Spirit to rightly divide between your soul and spirit realm. Let's look at Hebrews 4:12 again to see the value of meditating on His Word:

Hebrews 4:12
For the word of God is living and active and full of power
[making it operative, energizing, and effective]. It is sharper
than any two-edged sword, penetrating as far as the division of
the soul and spirit [the completeness of a person], and of both
joints and marrow [the deepest parts of our nature], exposing
and judging the very thoughts and intentions of the heart.

If we examine the five precious chapters in First John, we can see John explaining how beautiful and glorious Jesus is and that he (and many others) has seen Jesus with his own eyes. John speaks of God's pure light and how Jesus' Blood covers all of our unrighteousness. Chapter two describes how we can tell a phony Christian, and in the same chapter, we are encouraged by the truth that our sins are permanently removed. We are reminded that we have a relationship with the God of the universe, and that we have already defeated the evil one. He admonishes us to not love the world, but believe in Jesus and embrace the truth because it contains power. Chapters three and four further establish God's love for us and remind us to love one another. Chapter five speaks of our secure salvation and that we are victorious and have overcome the world. One of the key Scriptures in chapter four that has helped some of my clients in tearing down OCD fearful thoughts is 1 John 4:18-19:

1 John 4:18-19 Amplified Bible (AMP)
18 There is no fear in love [dread does not exist]. But perfect
(complete, full-grown) love drives out fear, because fear involves [the
expectation of divine] punishment, so the one who is afraid [of God's
judgment] is not perfected in love [has not grown into a sufficient
understanding of God's love]. 19 We love, because [a]He first loved us.

This Scripture can be used as a prescription for overcoming fear. Each time someone suffering with OCD (or fear in general) has a fearful thought that they recognize in their mind, if they apply this Scripture to the fear, they can be successful in casting the fear out.

For example, if a person has a fear thought that says, "If I don't pray today God will be mad at me or He might not love me." We then read (and apply) the above Scripture and cast that fear down by seeing clearly that this is an immature thought produced through a spirit of fear. We see that this fear is producing an irrational thought that God will not love us. The Scripture clearly tells us that we do not need to fear divine punishment as a result of not doing something for a day. This is a self-imposed rule, not a God-imposed rule. This produces guilt, fear, condemnation and, anxiety. Is it good to read Scripture daily? Of course, but it's not a deal-breaker with God.

Another example would be when people believe that they got sick or have an illness because they were punished by God. If we experience an illness or disease, it is not the result of God's wrath. We are under the Blood of Christ. It may be from the choices that we have made with our bodies or minds or it may even be the result of our environment or how we were raised as a child, but it is certainly not because God smote us with something horrible because He is angry. There is a spiritual law that God put into the world when He created it called "reaping and sowing". Basically, what you sow (or have been exposed to against your will) that is negative, toxic, or destructive will have negative consequences. These issues need to be confessed and repented for in the shed Blood of Jesus. Then we must choose to release any bad habits, toxic thinking and emotions from our past and current lives by surrendering these things to the Lord. Most of us know that once we repent of something as Christians, we are to partner with God and allow His Holy Spirit to assist us in achieving the positive, opposite results. Sometimes the results are immediate and sometimes this becomes a process that we walk through with God.

Proverbs 16:3 Amplified Bible (AMP)
3 [a]Commit your works to the Lord [submit and trust them to Him],
And your plans will succeed [if you respond
to His will and guidance].

Prayer: Dear Lord, I am realizing that I do not have to be victimized by OCD behaviors and propensities. I ask You to reveal to me through your precious Holy Spirit what steps as outlined in this chapter will help me to achieve victory in my mind and actions. I know that this will be a peaceful process filled with much insight because I am partnering with You. In Jesus' Name, amen.

Declaration: I decree and declare that according to Romans 8:37, that I am more than a conqueror in Christ Jesus. I will gain overwhelming victory through Him who loves me!

Romans 8:37 Amplified Bible (AMP)
37 Yet in all these things we are more than conquerors
and gain an overwhelming victory through Him
who loved us [so much that He died for us].

CHAPTER 5

Grief

1 Thessalonians 4:13
[The Hope of the Resurrection] And now, dear brothers and sisters,
we want you to know what will happen to the believers who
have died so you will not grieve like people who have no hope.

In this chapter, we are examining the roots of the spirit in terms of human loss. I am well acquainted with grief. As I sit here writing this the day after the third anniversary of my husband's unexpected death, I am certain that grief comes in waves just like the ebb and flow of the ocean by the shore. When we receive the news of someone's passing, we may feel like the whole weight of their loss is upon us, but I believe that God loves us too much to allow that. The grief cycle is designed to slowly allow our mind, will, emotions, and physical body to catch up with the reality that someone is gone until we have reached the acceptance stage of that loss. There is no timeline on arriving at a place of acceptance and closing the cycle. At three years, I feel like I am finally getting there. This is different for each loss and each person who is experiencing the loss. Please do not judge others for the length of time they need to heal. It's only acceptable to address this issue with a grieving person if you feel that their grief is no longer healthy and they are truly stuck and struggling with an inability to function on a daily basis with severe depression, and/or suicidal thoughts.

For most of you who have experienced a close loss (i.e., parent, spouse, child), you know that one day (or one minute) you may be fine and then suddenly a wave of grief and loss comes in just like a wave crashing onto the shore. Of course, the most healing action you can take in that moment is to allow yourself to feel the emotion and process it by crying, talking to God or a friend, journaling, etc. The worst thing you can do is shovel and stuff the emotions away behind a closed door in your mind and heart. The more in tune you are to God the more you will be able to receive His direction on how to remove the roots of any unnecessary grief. Notice I said unnecessary grief. Grief is natural and God built this cycle into us so we could truly heal and go on with our lives after a loss.

Part of getting through the grief cycle is to understand it. These stages include denial, anger, bargaining, depression, and acceptance. First, we have shock and numbness or disbelief. Then comes anger. If you tend to be more passive/aggressive, you may not even realize that you are angry. Then comes bargaining which means your mind plays out scenarios of, "Maybe if we had just done this and so we could have avoided this death." This is so normal in the process of getting through a loss. It is normal to allow your mind to go there as long as you don't camp there and cause yourself guilt or blame shift someone else's death onto another person. Perhaps you are blaming a doctor for not being capable of saving your loved one's life. Another example of blame shifting can manifest due to someone not taking care of themselves properly or an inexperienced driver was the possible cause of a car accident. We know there are times when, in situations like murder, someone else is to blame. Then it is more important to walk out forgiveness in the bargaining stage of grief so you can move on with your life in peace. The fourth stage is depression and that does not mean that you have to be in "I can't get out of bed" depression. In fact, the more you can stay out of any self pity the better the chances are that you won't end up in that type of pit.

Because of my awareness of the grief cycle, when I noticed any thoughts of self-pity rising up I would quickly allow God to pull me out. I refused to let myself go into vicim mode or wallow in self-pity. That's not an option when you know you have responsibilities. The fifth stage is acceptance. This is where you close the cycle on your grief. That does not mean that you forget the person or act as though they never existed. This means you can truly, fully move on with life without the grief holding you back. Some people get stuck here because they somehow feel that this is dishonoring to the person who passed away. It's quite the opposite. If your loved one was a believer, you know that they are in glory and the only thing that they want for you is to recognize that you are still on this planet for a reason and a purpose. You have a full life to live and it's not honoring to their memory or to God to stay stuck for them. It's actually dishonoring. If they could speak to you they would tell you how wrong it is to wallow. You may not realize this but there is actually an unholy spirit of grief (not normal grief) that can take people down a path to their own self-destruction. It also opens them up to the spirit of death and suicide if they are not careful.

If you stay as connected to God as possible during the processing of your loss, He will give you direction (keys) to pulling up some roots this will assist you in getting through your loss in the most healthy manner possible. In the rest of this chapter, I will be sharing some very personal keys that God gave me to lessen my own grief and keep the enemy out of my grieving process along the way. Some of them may be shocking to you and, believe me, I took some tongue lashings from others about some of the steps that I took. Do you know what? I don't care at all because I knew I was following God's instructions for MY life and I knew how much the pulling out of these roots gave me relief; so, I really didn't care at all about their opinions. When someone dies, everyone suddenly considers themselves a grief expert in your life and tries to tell you how to do it. I have made this mistake with others myself and have regretted it.

I hope that these steps will help those who currently feel stuck or maybe just need some hope that they don't have to stay stuck in their loss forever. Below is a timeline of where God took me personally in the sudden loss of my husband. This is not a formula. I am sharing my own experience to help you open yourself up to the Holy Spirit for any unique and personal instruction He gives you to help you along the way.

Day 1 (day of death) - remove trauma from the day.

My son and I had to perform CPR after finding his precious dad on the couch in the morning. My spouse had been dead for what appeared to be many hours. This was quite traumatic for us. If you have ever experienced any type of emergency where your adrenaline was pumping and your whole body seemed to jump into high gear, you will understand a level of what we experienced that morning. As an inner healer (counseling technique that removes trauma, pain, etc. from past experiences) I knew those first crucial moments needed some prayer before we went to bed that night in order for the trauma not to set in. We had our dear friend pray over the images and trauma from the morning's events until they seemed almost like a dream. You may be wondering what kind of prayer can hold this type of power. A prayer that goes back to the moment in time (of the traumatic event) and allows the blood of Jesus to cover the traumatic images and fight or flight mode that your body experiences.

If you are asking yourself how a prayer like that can go back in time and cover an event, it is based on the fact that we cannot time travel but the Holy Spirit and the blood of Jesus can.

2 Peter 3:8 (NLT) "But you must not forget this one thing, dear friends: A day is like a thousand years to the Lord, and a thousand years are like a day."

God is not in time. He is in eternity and is not limited by space and time since He created it. He has the power to cover any past trauma and wound. We just need to know and understand our authority in Christ and pray accordingly. The prayer may go something like this:

Dear Lord,

Thank You for the power and authority that You have given us in Jesus Christ. I now break the agreement and renounce any trauma, fear, etc (name each feeling that you want to remove) that I experienced at the moment of (name the incident or accident that occurred). I tell it to leave my body now in the Name of Jesus and I loose the peace and love of my Father God in its place. I cover the entire event in the blood of Jesus and I ask You, Holy Spirit, to resurrect anything that died inside of me (i.e., hope, belief, joy) that I need to live my life in a powerful way. In Jesus' Name, I pray. Amen.

You may also find it helpful to clap near your left ear as you begin this prayer. This opens up the emotional memory bank where all of that negative emotion is stored. It assists you in releasing that stored emotion and replacing it with something peaceful such a joy, hope, love.

Day 2: remove any guilt over discord in the relationship

One of the areas that the survivor from being a couple suffers during his/her grief cycle is regret. No relationship is perfect and we all have areas in our marriages that God is still perfecting. So just like any other couple (even after twenty-five years), we were working on learning to love and communicate in better ways. We had discord when the daily stresses of having two kids and a sick parent living with us, or everyday work, and ministry would take their toll. Because we could argue with the best of them, I received prayer that next day to release myself from any guilt, shame or condemnation that my mind or the enemy would try to heap on top of me in the grieving days that were ahead of me. I did not purposely seek this prayer out as I was in shock from the prior day. God in His great mercy met me where I was that next morning in the kitchen and allowed one of my dearest friends to pray over me so that regret from our past would not be fuel for condemnation to set in. The prayer was so powerful. That prayer was so effective that afterward, I was able to look at our relationship and how I could have been a better wife without condemnation. As the years have passed by I have been able to do this with no guilt or sorrow over what could have been. It helped me to glean the life lessons from our marriage without regret!

Here is an example of what that prayer could look like: *Dear Lord, as a follower of Christ I know that all sin has been paid for by You at the cross. I receive your forgiveness and apply it to any area of my marriage (can also cover any other close relationship including parents, children, siblings, friends, etc) that would cause me to have shame, guilt, condemnation or regret as I walk through this natural grieving process. In Jesus' name, Amen.*

Day 8 - day after funeral - removed engagement ring

One of the worst days for me personally was the day after the funeral. Of course, it had been one of the most surreal weeks of my life and I was exhausted and raw with so many emotions. It was a Sunday morning and my precious mom was staying with me for support. We managed to get a live stream of her local church service and we were listening to the opening worship music when God very clearly called me to go to my room because He had some things to speak to me. Now what I am going to share next may seem odd to some of you but I have learned in my walk with God that He can do whatever He wants and will do what's best for me as an individual. As I nestled myself into a chair in my room, I closed my eyes and waited for His presence. Suddenly I was taken up in a vision with Jesus on His throne and my husband was standing behind Him. They both began to tell me to remove my engagement ring. I found this so sudden and so odd; yet, as Jesus began to explain why biblically it made so much sense.

Jesus began to explain that, Hebraically, one is betrothed to the other upon engagement, not when the marriage ceremony takes place.

Here is what biblicaltruth.info has to say about this often misunderstood word:

Betrothal was an act of spousal or engagement for the purpose of marriage and appears to have been as binding as marriage itself (Genesis 19:14, Exodus 22:16-17, Deuteronomy 22:23-29, Hosea 2:19-20, Matthew 1:18). The word betroth occurs thirteen times in the Old Testament and the word espouse occurs once in the Old Testament and four times in the New Testament. The Hebrew word aras that is translated betroth nine times in the Old Testament is also translated espouse in II Samuel 3:14. Betrothal is a solemn promise of marriage, and it actually became a part of the marriage tradition, even though it was not marriage itself. According to Deuteronomy 20:7, a betrothed man was exempted from military service in order to take his wife and live with her,.

Please note that he had betrothed a wife but had not actually taken her in marriage. The commitment of betrothal was made long before they began living together as husband and wife. The word troth means the trust of marriage and the prefix be denotes nearness or closeness, meaning to cause to come to pass. The betrothed man was at times called a husband and the woman was called a wife even though they were not yet living together in marriage (Deuteronomy 22:23-24).

Jesus was telling me that the engagement was when the legal binding agreement really happened between my husband and me. I have no idea how long I sat in that chair sobbing at the thought of removing my engagement ring so soon, yet I know that God is always asking me to do things for my own good. When I was finally able to get that ring off of my finger, I put it into my fireproof box and immediately slipped my wedding ring back into its place on my finger. I must tell you that there was an instantaneous feeling of relief that washed over me. A layer of despair had left my soul as I removed the symbol of my betrothal. Please understand that it was not what I wanted to do, but what I knew was an instruction for my emotional benefit. I was truly blessed by this instruction which was such an act of love by my Heavenly Father! I felt so loved, cared for and cherished as I was given some pain relief as the surviving spouse. There was also one other component to this instruction that I believe was important. That component is the prophetic significance of numbers. My husband was buried on the seventh day after his death. Seven is the number of completion. So this completed his life on earth symbolically by burial. God asked me to remove the ring on the eighth day after my husband's death. Eight is the biblical number of new beginnings. Whether I liked it or not, that Sunday was a new beginning for me and it was so symbolic for me to remove that ring.

Day 38 removal of wedding ring.

I know day thirty-eight sounds seriously early to some of you to remove a wedding ring. Before my experience, I would have agreed with you, but one morning after dropping my daughter off at school, I felt the Holy Spirit ask me to take a ride. I went home to pray and confirm the destination which was about one hour from my home. I prepared myself, got into the car and began to drive and pray. I had not gotten very far when God asked me to count the number of days in my mind that it had been since I removed my engagement ring. It was for thirty days. He then began to speak to me about the significance of that number in the grieving cycle as it lines up with His Word. Both Aaron and Moses were mourned by the children of Israel for thirty days.

Numbers 20:29 Amplified Bible (AMP)
**29 When all the congregation saw that Aaron had died, all
the house of Israel wept (mourned) for him thirty days.**

When God would instruct Israel to take over territory and leave the women and children in Israel's care, He would specifically tell them not to touch any of the women, but to leave them to mourn their loss for thirty days first. God built something into us about mourning the first thirty days after a loss that is sacred to Him and quite profound.

Deuteronomy 21:10-13 Amplified Bible (AMP)
**10 "When you go out to battle against your enemies, and the
Lord your God hands them over to you and you lead them away**

captive, 11 and you see a beautiful woman among the captives, and desire her and would take her as your wife, 12 then you shall bring her [home] to your house, and she shall shave her head and trim her nails [in preparation for mourning]. 13 She shall take off the clothes of her captivity and remain in your house, and weep (mourn) for her father and her mother a full month. After that, you may go into her and be her husband and she shall be your wife.

As I drove toward my destination, God asked me to remove the wedding band and cut the soul tie that I had with my husband. A soul tie is a bond in the spirit that two people share through intercourse and their intense emotional bonds as they share intimate details of their lives with each other. I understood why my destination was so far away because it took me almost the entire ride to submit my will to the Father's will. Knowing His faithfulness to me, I knew it must be what was best for me even though I didn't feel ready for this step. I wasn't just crying at this point but was also groaning in despair. I had to pull over as it was no longer safe to drive the car. I pulled over into the nearest parking lot of a bar and grill that was empty and would not be open for a few hours. In that empty parking lot, I broke the soul tie with my husband and moved my wedding ring from the left ring finger to the right ring finger. I couldn't take it completely off of my body yet. It didn't feel right. Once again, as I yielded my will to His, another layer of unnecessary grief left me!

I felt the gentle voice of the Holy Spirit say, "look up at the name of this bar and grill." When I looked up I saw that its name was "Victory"! It was no accident that I parked in a place called Victory. It's not often that I pass by that little place but, when I do, I smile and remember God's faithfulness to me.

Some of you may have lost a spouse (or even divorced a spouse) but have not considered the soul tie you share. If you are remarried or considering remarriage, it would be beneficial to your next relationship to break the soul tie. If you have had many partners, it's also great for yourself and your spouse (present or future) to cut the soul ties with everyone else that you have had sex with. Here is the prayer that I use in the counseling office: (The first two sentences of the prayer only apply if you have had pre-marital sex.)

Dear Lord,

Forgive me for having sex outside of the marriage bed. I also choose to forgive myself. I now break every unhealthy and unholy emotional tie I knit with _____(fill in his/her name) and I break it in Jesus name. I also break the soul tie I knit with _____(fill in his/her name) in Jesus name and I command his/her piece of the soul out of me and back to _____(fill in name) and I command my piece of my soul back from _____(fill in his/her name), washed in the blood of Jesus, and back to me in Jesus Name.

I decree and declare purity and healing over my soul realm in Jesus' Name, Amen.

After praying this prayer, many people feel depression, oppression, and different types of hindrances leave them if they have had destructive relationships in the past. Breaking the soul tie also alleviates a level of emotional pain due to unwanted breakups. It helps to relieve the pain of grief as well as helps to cut down the number of dreams you have about someone from your past. Have you ever dreamt about a boyfriend or girlfriend from the past and then felt lingering feelings for them that next day? It's because of the soul tie. It's best to remove the spiritual tie and get the pieces of your soul back utilizing prayer and your authority in Christ.

Month # 9 - Removed his clothes from our closet.

This may seem trivial but anyone who has had to do this task understands what an act of permanency this symbolizes. Prophetically the number nine is the largest number indicating finality and completeness. If we think about the spiritual significance of the number nine, we see that many cycles in our lives run on a nine-month course. We see that most school years run approximately nine months (give or take a few weeks including breaks). We also know that pregnancy from conception to birth takes nine months for humans. Many times when you look back over the inception of a problem in your life, you will begin to birth the answers around the nine-month mark.

I felt the Lord encourage me to get this task completed before the ninth month was over. Since grief tends to peak at three, six and nine months in the first year, this was much harder than anticipated. I procrastinated a bit but managed to complete the assignment and donate much to good causes just one week past my perceived due date from God. Again, this was helpful in assisting me with another layer of grief falling away. I believe this step is so significant due to all of the memories that flood your mind as different articles of clothing bring back "moments in time". Perhaps there is a dress your wife wore when you went out for date night or your husband's favorite golf shirt brings back smiles as well as the pain of loss. Cleaning out the closet is like a counseling session (or many sessions) with God.

3 years - Write a goodbye letter to close the grief cycle

You may be surprised to see such a long space of time between my timeline from nine months to three years. The bottom line to that is just that the God-ordained grief cycle can take time. It can take much longer than my timeline as well; especially if you have not recognized the leading of the Holy Spirit to assist you with some unnecessary roots that can be cut off in their perfect timing. The goodbye letter is something I learned about in my days in counseling class. The letter gets written to the person whom you have lost. You write the letter as though they are standing right in front of you and you can say anything that you need or want to. You can tell them how much you miss them, what you are sad about what they will miss in the future, what you have anger about. Basically, whatever flows out of your fingertips onto paper is what you write. It doesn't matter if it is one page or one hundred pages. What matters is that you truly empty your heart for that person onto paper. It's healthier to write about the good as well as the bad. This is honesty time! This is not the time to paint a picture of perfection about your life or relationship with them. This is reality time penned onto paper. So many people practically idolize someone after they die; yet, they complained about them all of the time when they were here on earth. The bottom line is you are the one left here to continue your life and you need to get real on paper. The last line should include any forgiveness that needs to be extended to them as well as goodbye and I'll see you in heaven. If you are unsure about their salvation, please write about that in your goodbye statement as well.

This letter is so cleansing; yet, there is still one final step. You need to read the letter out loud to someone whom you trust with your heart. This closes the grieving cycle for most people. Why is this step of reading the letter out loud to someone else necessary? We are designed to be interdependent with others. We were never meant to isolate. It's also quite humbling to have others hear your heart poured out onto paper! I believe it lines up with this Scripture:

James 5:16 Amplified Bible (AMP)
16 Therefore, confess your sins to one another [your false steps, your
offenses], and pray for one another, that you may be healed and
restored. The heartfelt and persistent prayer of a righteous man
(believer) can accomplish much [when put into action and made
effective by God—it is dynamic and can have tremendous power].

Romans 12:5 Amplified Bible (AMP)
so we, who are many, are [nevertheless just] one
body in Christ, and individually [we are] parts one of
another [mutually dependent on each other].

When God spoke clearly to me to have this letter completed and shared with trusted friends before the three year anniversary of my husband's death, I chose very carefully. I chose friends who would be able to hear my heart without judging me for my thoughts and feelings. When I completed reading the letter out loud, they prayed over me for the cycle to be completed and declared over my life that my period of grieving had ended. I immediately felt a blanket of peace cover me that was so beautiful and sweet. I felt a bit of lingering grief for a few days afterward, but then I began to feel a huge shift in my whole being regarding the worst loss of my life. I felt more free and normal (my new normal) than I had felt in three years.

I will be forever grateful to the Lord for carrying me through the most traumatic experience of my life thus far! I have an inner knowing that this process would have looked much different if I had not been in tune to His leading throughout those first three years. My late husband is on my mind often; yet softly, safely he remains in the distance for the sake of my emotional health and my future.

Prayer and declaration over your life: *I decree and declare that my time of mourning has ended according to Isaiah 61:3. I am embracing the oil of joy in exchange for my mourning. I will trust and rely on the Lord and acknowledge His ways as I move forward in newness of life.*

Isaiah 61: 3 Amplified Bible (AMP)
3 To grant to those who mourn in Zion the following:
To give them a [a]turban instead of dust [on
their heads, a sign of mourning],
The oil of joy instead of mourning,
The garment [expressive] of praise instead of a disheartened spirit.
So they will be called the trees of righteousness
[strong and magnificent, distinguished for integrity,
justice, and right standing with God],
The planting of the Lord, that He may be glorified.

Proverbs 3:5-6Amplified Bible (AMP)
5 Trust in and rely confidently on the Lord with all your heart
And do not rely on your own insight or understanding.
6 [a]In all your ways know and acknowledge and recognize Him,
And He will make your paths straight and smooth
[removing obstacles that block your way

Chapter 6

The Wilderness Experience

Joshua 1:5 Amplified Bible (AMP)
5 No man will [be able to] stand before you [to oppose you]
as long as you live. Just as I was [present] with Moses, so
will I be with you; I will not fail you or abandon you.

If you have been around Christians long enough, you know that "wilderness" describes times when you are in a dry or what feels like a dark or difficult place. You may be dealing with a financial, spiritual, emotional, mental, or physical attack. This experience can often feel as though it will never end. It can seem like God is nowhere to be found and sometimes even your family and friends don't really understand the depth of what you are experiencing.

I had the unpleasant opportunity of going through a short wilderness experience recently and was so grateful that it only lasted a month! I had also been given a prophetic word days prior to that spiritual attack that I was about to go into a test.

Within three days of that prophetic word, an accusation questioning my motives over a decision that I made came forth. It was the first time in my remembrance that other people witnessing the event saw the unholy assignment (and its accompanying unholy spirits) release over me in the spirit realm. It took me completely off guard and I was wide open to this attack. Due to past experiences, I knew immediately that how I reacted and/or responded to this event was imperative.

Just a few days later during this short but intense trial, my daughter and I were out of town on a brief camping trip. I was crying out to God for Him to speak to me regarding this whole situation. It felt like one of the worst spiritual attacks in memory. I opened the Bible randomly and asked God to speak to me. Many call this Bible roulette. I opened to the book of Matthew chapter one which gives the genealogy from Abraham to Jesus. I couldn't see one reason why this would speak to me but I went ahead and read it anyway. As I finished, I asked God what that had to do with my situation. He simply spoke to my spirit that what we birth in the wilderness or captivity times in our lives determines what we birth when we are on the mountain top (when things are going good). Wilderness experiences tend to come after mountaintop experiences. This is in essence a diagram of what was birthed during the best and the worst of those times in the forty-two generation lineage of Jesus. Let's look at that list of these men and women:

Matthew 1 Amplified Bible (AMP)
The Genealogy of Jesus the Messiah
1 The record of the genealogy of [a]Jesus the [b]Messiah, the son
(descendant) of [c]David, the son (descendant) of Abraham:
2 Abraham [d]was the father of Isaac, Isaac the father of Jacob,
and Jacob the father of [e]Judah and his brothers [who became the
twelve tribes of Israel]. 3 Judah was the father of Perez and Zerah
by Tamar, Perez was the father of Hezron, and Hezron the father
of Ram. 4 Ram was the father of Aminadab, Aminadab the father
of Nahshon, and Nahshon the father of Salmon. 5 Salmon was the
father of Boaz by [f]Rahab, Boaz was the father of Obed by Ruth, and
Obed the father of Jesse. 6 Jesse was the father of [g]David the king.
David was the father of Solomon by [h]Bathsheba who had been the
wife of Uriah. 7 Solomon was the father of Rehoboam, Rehoboam
the father of Abijah, and Abijah the father of Asa. 8 Asa was
the father of Jehoshaphat, Jehoshaphat the father of Joram, and
Joram the father of Uzziah. 9 Uzziah was the father of Jotham,
Jotham the father of Ahaz, and Ahaz the father of Hezekiah.
10 Hezekiah was the father of Manasseh, Manasseh the father
of Amon, and Amon the father of Josiah. 11 Josiah became the
father of Jeconiah [also called Coniah and Jehoiachin] and his
brothers, at the time of the deportation (exile) to Babylon.
12 After the deportation to Babylon: Jeconiah became the father of
Shealtiel, and Shealtiel the father of Zerubbabel. 13 Zerubbabel was
the father of Abihud, Abihud the father of Eliakim, and Eliakim the
father of Azor. 14 Azor was the father of Zadok, Zadok the father
of Achim, and Achim the father of Eliud. 15 Eliud was the father
of Eleazar, Eleazar the father of Matthan, and Matthan the father
of Jacob. 16 Jacob was the father of Joseph the husband of Mary,
by [i]whom Jesus was born, who is called the Messiah (Christ).
17 So all the generations from Abraham to David are fourteen; from
David to the Babylonian deportation (exile), fourteen generations; and
from the Babylonian deportation to the Messiah, fourteen generations.

You probably noticed that the number fourteen is mentioned in verse seventeen three times. There are a few prophetic meanings for the number fourteen. The first one is "salvation" and "deliverance." Another is "double spiritual perfection." Even though I am not writing about those meanings, it may be something that you want to explore with the Lord yourself. There is much revelation to be had just in verse seventeen.

Let's focus on two verses of Matthew chapter one:

11 Josiah became the father of Jeconiah [also called Coniah and Jehoiachin] and his brothers, at the time of the deportation (exile) to Babylon. 12 After the deportation to Babylon: Jeconiah became the father of Shealtiel, and Shealtiel the father of Zerubbabel.

Let's take a look at what these names mean and perhaps this may help to paint a picture of the seventy years the Israelites spent in exile. Josiah means "Jehovah will raise." He fathered Jeconiah which means "Yah will establish." Shealtiel was birthed next and his name means "I have asked God." Sheatiel was the father of Zerubbabel. His name means "the seed of or conceived in Babylon (confusion)." We know that names have much meaning (especially in the Word) and that they can paint a picture for us which reveals a deeper spiritual meaning. In this Scripture, I know that God raised Josiah for the time when the Israelites were being led into exile (the wilderness). I also see that the first offspring, Josiah, carried a promise to establish and give them a life while they were in exile. With the birth of Sheatiel came a deeper crying out and asking of God for deliverance from exile. By the fourth generation, we see that Zerubbabel's name could imply that they were in the midst of confusion due to the lack of godly direction and instruction. If you know the story, it wasn't until God called them back to Jerusalem and they built the wall, that they once again re-opened the Book of the Law of Moses and learned the ways of the Lord again. It's so interesting the the Word can be quite cyclical (we have been experiencing the same thing in the USA for decades).

I am sure you will be able to see the parallels in these verses:

Nehemiah 4:7-9 Living Bible (TLB)
7 But when Sanballat and Tobiah and the Arabians, Ammonites, and Ashdodites heard that the work was going right ahead and that the breaks in the wall were being repaired, they became furious. 8 They plotted to lead an army against Jerusalem to bring about riots and confusion. 9 But we prayed to our God and guarded the city day and night to protect ourselves.

Notice how at that that time Babylon and the other enemies of the Israelites were trying to bring confusion and chaos into their lives. Remember Babylon means confusion.

Now, let's take this down to a personal level. When we are about to be further established in our faith or position of authority, the enemy will surely come at us. However, he too has to count the cost. He knows if we pass the test, we will be further established in Christ.

Sometimes wilderness experiences tend to come after mountaintop experiences and sometimes they seemingly come out of nowhere and for no particular reason. Why? We can speculate and say perhaps it is to keep us humble or develop fruit, or to keep us full of gratitude when things are good. On the other hand, we can become desperate for God to deliver us when things are bad and we find ourselves in the wilderness. No matter what, God loves us. He knows what experiences will produce Kingdom fruit in our lives if we allow Him. Although I do not believe that God afflicts us with things such as cancer, poverty, etc. We do live in a sinful, fallen world and stuff happens. Sometimes stuff happens because of our choices and sometimes we are experiencing the consequence of other people's choices. However, the Word does say that we will experience tests and trials.

Regardless of why we are in a situation, be it short-lived or for an extended period of time, there is something we can birth in exile that is worth enduring the wilderness time. God does not waste our time. One of my counseling teachers used to say that we can learn something from each and every situation we are in; even if the reason we are in the wilderness is due to someone else's sin. She used to say that there is a reason why we are on the receiving end of what's happening even if we did not cause the situation. We can learn something from each experience.

Romans 8:28 Amplified Bible (AMP)
28 And we know [with great confidence] that God [who
is deeply concerned about us] causes all things to work
together [as a plan] for good for those who love God, to those
who are called according to His plan and purpose.

We can waste our time if we spend that time not taking responsibility for ourselves while in the wilderness. One of the most important lessons we can glean in the wilderness is to find more of our identity in Jesus. We tend to learn much about our strengths but mostly about our weaknesses while enduring a trial or wilderness time.

Let's look at the ultimate example which Jesus Christ Himself left us during His wilderness time just after He was baptized. We know that the Word says that the Spirit drove Him out into the wilderness after John baptized Him with water.

Matthew 4 Amplified Bible (AMP)
The Temptation of Jesus
*4 Then Jesus was led by the [Holy] Spirit into the wilderness to
be tempted by the devil. 2 After He had gone without food for
forty days and forty nights, He became hungry. 3 And the tempter
came and said to Him, "If You are the Son of God, command that
these stones become bread." 4 But Jesus replied, "It is written
and forever remains written, 'Man shall not live by bread alone,
but by every word that comes out of the mouth of God.'"
5 Then the devil took Him into the holy city [Jerusalem]
and placed Him on the pinnacle (highest point) of the
temple. 6 And he said [mockingly] to Him, "If You are the
Son of God, throw Yourself down; for it is written,
'He will command His angels concerning You [to
serve, care for, protect and watch over You]';*
and
*'They will lift You up on their hands,
So that You will not strike Your foot against a stone.'"
7 Jesus said to him, "On the other hand, it is written and forever
remains written, 'You shall not test the Lord your God.'"
8 Again, the devil took Him up on a very high mountain and
showed Him all the kingdoms of the world and the glory [splendor,
magnificence, and excellence] of them; 9 and he said to Him, "All
these things I will give You, if You fall down and worship me."
10 Then Jesus said to him, "Go away, Satan! For it is written and
forever remains written, 'You shall worship the Lord your God,
and serve Him only.'" 11 Then the devil left Him; and angels came
and ministered to Him [bringing Him food and serving Him].*

When we read over these well-known passages, we see that the Holy Spirit led Jesus into the wilderness, thereby confirming that our testing can come from God. We also see that He endured a forty-day period of fasting. The number forty often lines up with a time of testing in the Bible. We see that after that, Satan came at Jesus with every thing he had just to see what Jesus was made of. Herein lies our root of the spirit that God revealed to me about two years ago. God reminded me that for thirty years Jesus was identified just as the son of a carpenter (Joseph). Father God saw fit to take the forty days in the wilderness to speak to His Son (Jesus). I believe that during that time, Father God was stripping away Jesus' identity as only a carpenter's son and fully activating Him as the Son of the most High God. I believe that Jesus may not have been able to pass the test of

Satan's three commands when Satan came against Him had He not been fully activated into His identity as the Son of the most High God.

During my recent one-month wilderness experience, it appeared to most involved that I was one hundred percent on the receiving end of an undeserved spiritual attack. I mentioned before that a close confidant warned me of an upcoming test. I didn't want to receive that word. As it happened, It was one of the worst spiritual hits I had taken to date and I struggled greatly. I didn't feel as though I could trust anyone and I was surprised by what came at me spiritually during this time. The only two things I had the grace to handle were counseling my clients and praying. Worshiping God and reading His Word were the only things that brought me any solace. I would take my teacher's advice and ask God daily to remove all unhealthy attributes from my life so that I could avoid experiencing this ugly type of situation ever again. One of my favorite Scriptures is:

> **James 1:5 Amplified Bible (AMP)**
> **5 If any of you lacks wisdom [to guide him through a**
> **decision or circumstance], he is to ask of [our benevolent]**
> **God, who gives to everyone generously and without**
> **rebuke or blame, and it will be given to him.**

God was faithful to show me a thing or two that could be rooted out of my own identity that did not line up with who He says I am. As I broke agreement with those roots, I was then able to see why I was in such pain and an open target for this type of spiritual attack. You see when we are in exile for a long time, or in a period of testing for maybe a short time, there are things that God wants/needs to work out of us, provided we are coachable, teachable, and open to His Holy Spirit. If not, we can become mistrusting of others and greater targets for offense and allowing hurtful words to penetrate into our soul realm as a result of self-pity and self-centeredness. For example, if an ungodly assignment comes at you through a person from the enemy the first thing we immediately need to remember is what Paul says in Ephesians chapter six:

> **Ephesians 6:12-14 Amplified Bible (AMP)**
> **12 For our struggle is not against flesh and blood [contending**
> **only with physical opponents], but against the rulers, against**
> **the powers, against the world forces of this [present] darkness,**
> **against the spiritual forces of wickedness in the heavenly**
> **(supernatural) places. 13 Therefore, put on the complete armor**
> **of God, so that you will be able to [successfully] resist and**
> **stand your ground in the evil day [of danger], and having done**

*everything [that the crisis demands], to stand firm [in your place,
fully prepared, immovable, victorious]. 14 So stand firm and
hold your ground, having [a]tightened the wide band of truth
(personal integrity, moral courage) around your waist and having
put on the breastplate of righteousness (an upright heart),*

In these times if we have pride, false humility, self-pity and are focused on the sin of others, we are not open to attaining a greater place of freedom and deliverance from ourselves (the parts of your flesh nature that have not yet conformed into the image of Christ) we will not be able to come up higher into our identity in Jesus. As we mature in our relationships with others, it's imperative to remember that the way we experience an event is just one perspective in a given situation. If someone hurt us (the enemy used this person to get to us), that person most likely has a completely different perspective of the situation than we do. A very common phrase is, "Hurting people hurt people". Often times we experience the effects of someone else's fragile emotional state. They may be angry at someone else but we received the brunt of their fury. Maybe they have multiple unhealed wounds and unforgiveness from past events that remind them of the current event. Maybe they are full of pride and can never own their own sinful ways. There are many reasons why the other person or persons can react in an over-inflated way. This is a good time to try our best to put ourselves in the other person's shoes and even ask God to show us their perspective. Ask yourself and more importantly, ask God what is truth in this situation or testing according to Ephesians 6:14.

I will not be the person who says you are to enjoy your wilderness time. To me from my own human standpoint, I will say that it is not very realistic. I will say, however, to count it all joy when you are being more deeply identified as the child of God and further establishing yourself in Christ as a result of the trial.

Knowing that some wilderness experiences are short and some are extended, the key here is to remember that what we are birthing during this time will greatly determine what we birth when we are on the mountain top again. The wilderness time needs to establish us deeper in our love, commitment, maturity, and calling in Christ Jesus. Don't waste it blame-shifting or complaining. We may have to experience the same type of situation again if we do not learn what was imperative for us to grow up in Christ.

Declaration: I decree and declare that this time I am spending in the wilderness will produce much good fruit in my life. My God is faithful to prune the unfruitful branches according to John 15:2. I will learn everything I need to learn from this wilderness experience and I will be further established in Christ Jesus as a result of this testing.

John 15:2 Amplified Bible (AMP)
2 Every branch in Me that does not bear fruit, He takes away; and every branch that continues to bear fruit, He [repeatedly] prunes, so that it will bear more fruit [even richer and finer fruit].

Dear Lord Jesus,

When I am in the wilderness, may I always remember Your time of testing and know that If I humble myself under the mighty hand of God, I will find myself more deeply identifying with You, my Savior. Amen

Chapter 7

Spiritual soul ties

It is fitting to begin this chapter by exploring what a soul tie entails so we can have a greater understanding of how it affects our everyday lives. As most of you know, we are three part beings. The parts that make us up are body, spirit, and soul. Many people believe that our soul and spirit are the same thing. I personally believe they are not. I think that our spirit is what gets regenerated by the Holy Spirit upon our salvation. We still have a physical body and soul realm that is un-regenerated. Our soul consists of our unconscious, subconscious and conscious mind, our emotions, beliefs, attitudes, feelings, memories, personality and our self-will to make choices. The soul realm is a pretty complicated place if you ask me. Our soul determines to a great degree, what happens with our physical body. I believe when we die our spirit goes to be with God, provided we have made Jesus Lord.

I briefly mentioned soul ties in the chapter on grief, but in this chapter, we will take a deeper look at how they affect our lives. Soul ties are a knitting together in the soul realm that takes place when two people come together sexually. These bonds were created by God to unite a couple in marriage as one flesh.

I believe this soul exchange gives us a greater sense of loyalty to that person and in most cases causes us to be so much more in tune with what they are thinking and feeling.

In today's world where sex is no longer regarded as a sacred act to be enjoyed only in marriage, we can co-mingle our soul realms with many people, thereby losing a piece of ourselves each time we participate in a sexual soul exchange with a new partner.

The good news is that we have powerful prayers in the Body of Christ that can break that tie and release us from the other person's soul realm. Here is a prayer that a can be used to break any soul ties which may be lurking within your soul:

Dear Heavenly Father,

Please forgive me for having sex outside of marriage. I now break every unhealthy and unholy emotional tie I knit with _____(fill in their name) in Jesus' Name. I break the soul tie I knit with _____(fill in their name) and I command their piece of their soul out of me and back to them in Jesus' Name. I command my piece of my soul out of _____(fill in their name), washed in the Blood of Jesus, and back to me in Jesus' Name.

Pray this prayer for each person with whom you had relations if you want to be free from the soul tie. You can also pray this prayer for past marriages as well as for anyone whose name you do not remember. There can be many reasons for such a situation. You may have been sexually assaulted (you do not have to ask for forgiveness as sexual assault is not a choice) or had a past with drugs or alcohol and don't know and/or remember each person with whom you had an encounter. Please hear my heart, God knows who those people are. All you need to do is come before Him and pray this prayer, pouring your heart out about any of those unknown moments. He is faithful to set you free.

Proverbs 6:32
But whoever commits adultery with a woman lacks common
sense and sound judgment and an understanding [of moral
principles]; He who would destroy his soul does it.

Most people feel more freedom after they pray these prayers. They find that they stop dreaming about the person as well. Have you ever had a dream about a prior partner that you haven't seen for a long time and when you wake up, you seem somehow to have a residue of them on you? It's an odd feeling sometimes coupled with a little bit of rekindled feelings for them. Usually, by mid-day this feeling does wear off. This type of experience is due to the soul tie. Breaking the tie will clean up your dream state as well. If you dream about that person again, it will not leave you with any lingering feelings of attachment.

We can also knit a different kind of soul tie with very close friends.

Most of us know this biblical example:

1 Samuel 18 Amplified Bible (AMP)
Jonathan and David
18 When David had finished speaking to Saul, the soul of Jonathan
was bonded to the soul of David, and [a]Jonathan loved him as
himself. 2 Saul took David that day and did not let him return to
his father's house. 3 Then Jonathan made a covenant with David
because he loved him as himself. 4 Jonathan stripped himself
of the outer robe that he was wearing and gave it to David,
with his armor, including his sword, his bow, and his belt.

Unfortunately, some have tried to twist this Scripture to imply that David and Jonathan were lovers. This is not the case. These guys had each other's backs at a time when it was a matter of life or death for David. This is a picture of loyalty and being willing to lay one's life down for another person. The meaning of "loved" in verse 18 is "philio" or "phileo" which means "brotherly love". This is the love that Christians are commanded to have for one another. Jesus said, "This is my commandment, that you love one another as I have loved you. Greater love has no one than this, that someone lay down his life for his friends. You are my friends if you do what I command you" (John 15:12-14). This love is very unselfish and is like the love soldiers display while under fire trying to save a fellow soldier who is wounded. Phileo love is love that displays a willingness to die or risk dying for someone or others in order to save or protect their lives.

We can certainly knit healthy, holy soul ties with friends and others as we share intimate details of our lives with them. We can also knit unhealthy ties as well. It's good to pray the above prayer (minus the line about having sex with them) if you have been betrayed or have broken off a friendship with someone who is no longer a part of your life. The prayer will keep your soul realm in a more emotionally healthy state.

There is another type of soul tie about which few people have written. This is a tie that can come when we allow the unhealthy, unholy things in our lives to gain too much of a place of authority in our soul realm. We can have a soul tie with an unholy spirit. The first time I discovered this was with a dear friend who was very much aware of all of her fears. She had been working consistently with the Lord to destroy this stronghold in her life. She had some success but not enough. We were having a conversation one day on the beach and she was sharing her frustration with still having so much fear. We began to pray and ask God for the Keys to the Kingdom of heaven to break this level of fear that was running her life.

> *Matthew 16:19 Amplified Bible (AMP)*
> *19 I will give you the keys (authority) of the kingdom of*
> *heaven; and whatever you bind [forbid, declare to be improper*
> *and unlawful] on earth [a]will have [already] been bound*
> *in heaven, and whatever you loose [permit, declare lawful]*
> *on earth [b]will have [already] been loosed in heaven."*

God showed us that she had a soul tie to the spirit of fear. I heard this phrase in my spirit, *"You can get so in bed with a spirit that you create a soul tie with it"*. I was blown away by this revelation. As my friend broke soul ties with the spirit of fear, on that hot, ninety-degree day, every hair stood up on her entire body. That was over a decade ago and she has not experienced that level of fear again.

Let's find some biblical basis for this belief based on the experiences of myself as well as the identical experiences of others.

> *1 Corinthians 10:14*
> *Therefore, my beloved, run [keep far, far away] from [any sort*
> *of] idolatry [and that includes loving anything more than God, or*
> *participating in anything that leads to sin and enslaves the soul].*

It's enlightening the way the Amplified Bible tells us that participating in idolatry enslaves the soul. In my friend's case, she was exalting fear above the Lord and idolizing it (or giving it more power).

> *James 1:21*
> *So get rid of all uncleanness and all that remains of wickedness, and*
> *with a humble spirit receive the word [of God] which is implanted*
> *[actually rooted in your heart], which is able to save your souls.*

If you are unfamiliar with the book of James, this first chapter is highlighting what a double-minded man is dealing with. James speaks much in chapter one about the things that afflict our soul realm and how to be set free. The above Scripture tells us that we are to humbly receive the Word of God which is able to save our souls. The word soul referenced here and in all New Testament Scriptures, is the Greek word "sa-ar". It can mean, to "grow stormier, rougher"; "to be enraged, to scatter in a wind, or driven with a whirlwind, sore troubled, tossed with a tempest". These references are clearly not talking about our spirit which is regenerated by the Holy Spirit upon salvation. It is referencing our emotions, will, etc.

Proverbs 21:10
The soul of the wicked desires evil [like an addictive
substance]; His neighbor finds no compassion in his eyes.

1 Thessalonians 5:23 Amplified Bible (AMP)
23 Now may the God of peace Himself sanctify you through
and through [that is, separate you from profane and vulgar
things, make you pure and whole and undamaged—
consecrated to Him—set apart for His purpose]; and may
your spirit and soul and body be kept complete and [be
found] blameless at the coming of our Lord Jesus Christ.

I want to share another story with you. I was working with a woman who had been exposed to a form of Christianity that was very legalistic. This church operated under so many unnecessary rules and regulations that she was held captive to rules and regulations her entire childhood. As she began to grow and think for herself, she began to question some of their interpretations of Scripture. Each time she would ask questions, she was labeled as rebellious and non-compliant. She also ended up feeling so condemned by the constant scrutiny that she began to lie often just to escape the interrogations and confrontations. As an adult, she left this cult-like church. After a year or so of counseling, she came to me with much depression. Apparently, she had been working with a wonderful counselor who had assisted her in getting much freedom back in Christ, however, she still experienced some mental torment. There were many layers of healing that this woman needed after growing up in that type of atmosphere.

On one particular visit with her, I felt totally incapable of helping her. I cried out to the Lord for His wisdom and He showed me something extraordinary. He showed me the inside of her mind. I could see a tiny demon sitting in there and when a thought from the enemy came in, the little demonic thing would open a trap door and allow the thought to come in. It would then close the door so that the thought could not get back out. I ask the Lord what this demon was. He very clearly stated "Rebellion". I was not sure how I was going to tell this woman that she had a stronghold of rebellion in her mind since this cultish church had accused her of that very thing when she would question their biblical interpretations. I was able to share what I saw with her and we determined that she had adopted and accepted what they told her (that she was rebellious) so often that she formed a deep tie with that spirit. As I led her in a prayer of asking God to forgive her for allowing that thing to be a part of her mind, she renounced that tie. We had also been given the instruction from God to have her *invite* the Holy Spirit into the area in her mind where this spirit of rebellion had been residing. We kicked rebellion out in the Name of Jesus and she then invited the Holy Spirit into her mind. What happened next was awesome! She physically felt rebellion leave and the Holy Spirit enter that place in her mind. As time passed, she was able to not only have more peace and less depression, but also she was able to discern the gentle conviction of the Holy Spirit and hear His thoughts for her life instead of carrying shame, guilt, and condemnation.

This was such a cool concept to me. Afterward, I decided to pray the prayer for myself as well. I believe that we can all benefit from a prayer like that. It is my belief that we all have some territory that we haven't fully given over to God. That means we have some rebellion going on in our minds. As I prayed the prayer, I felt a gentle rush and then noticed during the next few weeks that I also was recognizing and capturing thoughts in my head about which I was previously unaware. It was peaceful and helpful.

2 Corinthians 10:5 Amplified Bible (AMP)
5 We are destroying sophisticated arguments and every
exalted and proud thing that sets itself up against the
[true] knowledge of God, and we are taking every thought
and purpose captive to the obedience of Christ,

You may be questioning why we would have to invite the Holy Spirit into our minds. We still have our soul realm and physical body that we control. We need to invite Him in. He is not a spiritual bully. We must ask Him to occupy our minds and bodies. Invite the Holy Spirit into your everything! Ask Him to come into your body, mind, will, emotions, memories, etc. Give Him the authority to come into your day and your schedule as well. You won't be disappointed.

Hebrews 4:12 Amplified Bible (AMP)
12 For the word of God is living and active and full of power
[making it operative, energizing, and effective]. It is sharper than
any two-edged [a]sword, penetrating as far as the division of
the [b]soul and spirit [the completeness of a person], and of both
joints and marrow [the deepest parts of our nature], exposing
and judging the very thoughts and intentions of the heart.

When the thoughts and intentions of our hearts are exposed, we can then renounce any ungodly soul ties we have with whatever unholy attachment God is revealing. Here is an example of how one would pray this type of prayer.

Heavenly Father,

Please forgive me for getting so in bed with the spirit of _____(fill in name of the spirit, i.e, fear, jealousy, hatred, rebellion, etc.) that I have inadvertently knit a soul tie to it. I now break every soul tie(s) I knit with the spirit of _____(fill in name) and renounce having allowed that spirit to attach to my soul realm. I command it and all attachments to leave me now in Jesus' Name. Holy Spirit I invite you into that place in my soul realm where _____(fill in the blank, i.e., fear, jealousy, hatred, rebellion, etc.) had a stronghold and release Your perfect love in place in Jesus' Name, amen.

Declaration: I decree and declare that there will be no room in my soul for the enemy. I will love the Lord my God with all of my heart, mind, soul, and strength according to Deuteronomy 6:5. My entire being will run after God and I will not be distracted from the adoration that God has planted in my heart for Him.

Deuteronomy 6:5 Amplified Bible (AMP)
5 You shall love the Lord your God with all your heart and mind and with all your soul and with all your strength [your entire being].

Chapter 8

Deep calls out to deep

Job 10:12 Amplified Bible (AMP)
12 You have granted me life and lovingkindness;
And Your providence (divine care, supervision)
has preserved my spirit.

The longer we walk with God the quicker we recognize when God is speaking to us. Even as seasoned Christians oftentimes we assume what is running through our mind's are just our own thoughts. Later we realize it was the Lord speaking in a gentle, quiet voice which seemed as fleeting as a whisper.

1 Kings 19:11-12 The Message (MSG)
11-12 Then he was told, "Go, stand on the mountain at attention
before God. God will pass by. A hurricane wind ripped through
the mountains and shattered the rocks before God, but God wasn't
to be found in the wind; after the wind an earthquake, but God
wasn't in the earthquake; and after the earthquake fire, but God
wasn't in the fire; and after the fire a gentle and quiet whisper.

Most of us have had the experience of thinking about a person whom we haven't seen in years and suddenly they call us or appear at our same location within a few days of our having that original thought of them. I believe this is an occasion when God is speaking to our spirit-man but we are not in tune with our spirit enough to awaken to His voice. We usually think of these fleeting thoughts as coming from our own mind.

But is it just a coincidence when we have these thoughts prior to our encounters? I know that personally, upon salvation, my awareness of what I used to consider random thoughts and coincidences amped up exponentially. As I grew in Christ, I had more and more encounters where I knew I was on God's heavenly wavelength. For example, I had not seen a young woman whom I had been friendly with in my twenties for a few decades. God had been taking me on a journey of asking for forgiveness from all those whom I had wronged prior to salvation. She was on my heart. I had no contact with her and didn't know how to find her. I had to assume this was God's thought and not my own. I told God that if I owed her an apology, He should somehow make her appear in my life. I hadn't seen her in twenty-five years, however, within days of that prayer she friend requested me on social media. I promptly responded with a heartfelt apology which she accepted.

Most Christians I know personally share with me that they constantly question themselves regarding whether what they are thinking is coming from the Holy Spirit or from their own thoughts. I agree there are times when we are just thinking our own carnal thoughts, but we must be open to exploring the possibility that more thoughts are Holy Spirit led than we consciously discern. Let's examine some Scriptures which support this:

Romans 9:1 Amplified Bible (AMP)
9 I am telling the truth in Christ, I am not lying, my conscience testifies with me [enlightened and prompted] by the Holy Spirit,]

Hebrews 10:14-17 Amplified Bible (AMP)
14 For by the one offering He has perfected forever and completely cleansed those who are being sanctified [bringing each believer to spiritual completion and maturity]. 15 And the Holy Spirit also adds His testimony to us [in confirmation of this]; for after having said, 16 "This is the covenant that I will make with them After those days, says the Lord: I will imprint My laws upon their heart, And on their mind, I will inscribe them [producing an inward change],"

1 John 2:20 Amplified Bible (AMP)
20 But you have an anointing from the Holy One [you have been set apart, specially gifted and prepared by the Holy Spirit], and all of you know [the truth because He teaches us, illuminates our minds, and guards us from error].

1 John 2:27 Amplified Bible (AMP)
27 As for you, the anointing [the special gift, the preparation] which you received from Him remains [permanently] in you, and you have no need for anyone to teach you. But just as His anointing teaches you [giving you insight through the

> *presence of the Holy Spirit] about all things, and is true and*
> *is not a lie, and just as His anointing has taught you, [a]you*
> *must remain in Him [being rooted in Him, knit to Him].*

I love these Scriptures! They should produce a godly confidence inside of us that we can be Spirit-led on a daily basis. So what stops us from walking in the awareness of the Holy Spirit continually? I believe it is due to the fact that we are three-part human beings. We are a physical body, soul realm, (mind, will, emotions, memory) and spirit.

As mentioned in a previous chapter, our spirit becomes alive and regenerated upon salvation. When the Holy Spirit comes in and regenerates our spirit-man, we come alive and in touch with the Father, Son, and Holy Spirit. New believers, upon salvation, can relate to Romans 8:16 which says:

> **Romans 8:16 Amplified Bible (AMP)**
> *16 The Spirit Himself testifies and confirms together with our*
> *spirit [assuring us] that we [believers] are children of God.*

This Scripture speaks of that "inner knowing" that you are going to heaven when you die. That assurance is the Holy Spirit witnessing that blessed assurance to your own spirit. The longer I live, the more I realize how little most of us pay attention to our regenerated spirit. We pay attention when we know God is speaking clearly to us through the Scriptures, through other people, and through the inner witness of the Holy Spirit giving us personal instruction or direction. Many of us also pay attention to the prophetic voices that give us words of instruction, encouragement, and/or direction. But what about the daily directives which are coming through our own regenerated spirit-man that most of us just seem to ignore? Some churches can operate at only 66.6 percent as well, ignoring the Holy Spirit and only acknowledging the Father and the Son. They don't make room for the Holy Spirit. We can operate that same way as individual Christians. Many of us pay attention to our physical bodies and our soul realm (mind, will, emotions, and memory) and pretty much ignore what is happening in our spirit all day (which is regenerated by the Holy Spirit).

Let me give you some examples. Many years ago I had a Christian friend who was preparing her finances in such a way that was odd. She suddenly began to be concerned, as a married woman, as to which bank accounts carried her name solely and which bills, mortgage, etc. had her husband's name on them as well. She dedicated time to making sure that she personally was secure financially for no known reason. Her marriage appeared to be solid and stable. Finally, this woman's best friend said to her that she was acting as though she were preparing for divorce. Her best friend began to probe her to see if she was withholding information about the state of her marriage. My friend was completely unaware that she was exhibiting this type of behavior by her financial actions until it was brought to her attention. She assured her best friend that all was well within the marriage. Within just a few shorts weeks, she discovered that her husband was having an affair. I believe the Holy Spirit was speaking to her spirit. Was the Spirit preparing her to leave the marriage? Actually, no. Their marriage survived and thrived after the affair was exposed and they received godly counsel. I do believe that the Holy Spirit was witnessing a warning to her spirit that she was not fully understanding. So her response to her lack of understanding of what God was relaying to her spirit was to act out in fear with regard to her financial status. If she had been more in tune with her spirit by giving it as much attention as her physical body and soul realm, she may have realized that she needed to begin to question God about why she was feeling this need to get herself financially secure. She may have been able to intercede for her marriage earlier or perhaps ask her husband if he was unhappy in the marriage, etc. even before the affair was exposed.

Another example is from my own life. Two years prior to my husband's sudden death, I began to ask God to help me to love my husband the way he really deserved to be loved because I knew that we would not have forever to get this marriage right. We had a good marriage, but like most couples, we had areas that needed improvement. Those last two years of his life, I had an urgency in my spirit to fix what I hadn't been able to get right with my husband in the first twenty-three years of marriage. Even though I was working on this area of my life, I was still cognitively unaware of the urgency happening in my spirit. Two weeks before my husband died, we were attending a fund-raiser. It was a dinner and dancing event. My husband and I had danced a few slow dances together. As we danced to our last slow song, I buried my head into my husband's neck in a way of finality and desperation that actually shocked me as it was happening. I remember even asking myself what I was doing and why was I suddenly so emotional and clinging to him in an abnormal way for me. I quickly dismissed my emotion and questions and moved on with the evening never giving it another thought. About a week after his death, I remembered that night. I realized that my spirit knew it would be the last time we would ever dance together on this earth and my spirit was embracing that final moment with everything it had! I look on that moment now with awe and wonder as to how much information my spirit had that my physical body and soul realm was clueless about.

I believe our spirit man has a direct line to the throne room and access to the Kingdom of Heaven. Our spirit man deserves to be included much more often in our daily plans and not just when we know that the Holy Spirit is speaking to us through the inner witness that feels like an internal, audible, voice. I think God is speaking multiple plans into our spirit man and we walk around clueless about much of this activity. Have you ever had an unfortunate event and could see how God prepared you for that upcoming loss or trial? Much of this preparation is taking place in our spirit man. Here are two Scriptures to back up my thoughts.

John 16:13 Amplified Bible (AMP)
13 But when He, the Spirit of Truth, comes, He will guide you
into all the truth [full and complete truth]. For He will not
speak on His own initiative, but He will speak whatever He
hears [from the Father—the message regarding the Son], and
He will disclose to you what is to come [in the future].

John 14:17 Amplified Bible (AMP)
17 the Spirit of Truth, whom the world cannot receive
[and take to its heart] because it does not see Him or
know Him, but you know Him because He (the Holy Spirit)
remains with you continually and will be in you.

In contrast, I believe that there are certain things that we are not to have a full knowledge and cognitive awareness of until such events actually occur. It would be fearful to know that a car accident was looming on the horizon or that someone was going to die on a certain day or time. I believe that God does not want us to have full knowledge of certain upcoming events. I do believe, however, that we would be able to pray more effectively, be more adequately prepared for, and possibly even bypass some upcoming unfortunate situations if we were more in tune with what was happening in our spirit man. Perhaps this greater awareness would help us to live our lives more fully.

Matthew 11:25 Amplified Bible (AMP)
25 At that time Jesus said, "I praise You, Father, Lord of heaven
and earth [I openly and joyfully acknowledge Your great
wisdom], that You have hidden these things [these spiritual
truths] from the wise and intelligent and revealed them to infants
[to new believers, to those seeking God's will and purpose].

Prayer: Dear Lord, I am now realizing how much more awareness I could possess about what You are saying to me through my spirit man. Holy Spirit, I give You full permission to remove any hinderance(s) in my soul realm and/or physical body which keeps me from giving my spirit (which is regenerated by Your Holy Spirt) more credence and attention. Please help me to draw more heavenly information from my spirit man from this moment on. I ask this in Jesus' Name, amen.

Another really interesting discovery made by some believers is the concept that we possess some control over our own spirit. Jesus had control over His spirit when He was hanging on the cross.

Matthew 27:50 Amplified Bible (AMP)
50 And Jesus cried out again with a loud [agonized] voice, and gave
up His spirit [voluntarily, sovereignly dismissing and releasing
His spirit from His body in submission to His Father's plan].

Have you noticed that some people have the ability to hold on to their spirit as well? How many times have you heard stories of someone lying in a hospital bed waiting for a loved one to come and visit before they will die. We also hear of people who wait until their family leaves their bedroom or hospital room before giving up their spirit and passing away. These instances, which are many, tell us that we possess some power to rule our own spirit if the Lord allows.

It would make sense to me that we would have this same ability that Jesus had to give up His spirit. We know that we are to walk in the power and authority that Jesus walked in and we are to do even greater things.

John 14:12 Amplified Bible (AMP)
12 I assure you and most solemnly say to you, anyone who
believes in Me [as Savior] will also do the things that I do;
and he will do even greater things than these [in extent
and outreach], because I am going to the Father.

The other concept about our spirits which I find amazing is that our spirit can speak to another person's spirit as it is departing from our earthly body.

The first time I ever encountered this phenomena was when my own mother was dying. I had the privilege of being present in her room as she went home to be with the Lord. About what seemed like fifteen minutes or so before she took her last breath, I was sitting next to her reading a book. All of a sudden, many thoughts and emotions which were not common to me rose up in my spirit man like a mighty flood! It was quite overwhelming in a good way and came with such peace and joy! I began to ask to Lord in earnest (based on what was being spoken to my mind) to not allow me to die without fulfilling the call He had on my life. I was overwhelmed with the need to not allow fear, insecurity, or any other obstacle stop me from "jumping off of the cliff with God" when He called me to do great exploits for Him and for the Kingdom. Again, this was one of those moments where I was so surprised by the rush of what was happening in my spirit man. Not long after that moment, my mother took her last breath. Two days later I was sitting on the beach asking God about that moment. The Holy Spirit interrupted my prayer and shared that this moment in time was my mother's spirit speaking final encouragement and instructions into my spirit before she left the room. I was so surprised by what Holy Spirit said that I immediately replied back to Him that He would need to give me a Scripture to back this up. I heard the following Scripture immediately in my spirit man:

Psalm 42:7-8 Amplified Bible (AMP)
7 Deep calls to deep at the [thundering] sound of Your waterfalls;
All Your breakers and Your waves have rolled over me. 8 Yet the
Lord will command His lovingkindness in the daytime, And in the
night His song will be with me, A prayer to the God of my life.

What I believe God was conveying to me was that the deep of a man (his spirit) can also call out and speak to the deep of another man (their spirit) as they are leaving this earth. I was still a little skeptical so I asked for more confirmation. The next day I was having a conversation with a very wise, mature, believer in Christ. I had shared with her that my mother had passed away just three days ago. She shared with me that her best friend had died and, as she was passing, her spirit spoke to her leaving a quick and final instruction before leaving the room. This was just the confirmation I needed. I love it when God answers prayers so quickly. This confirmation came within twenty-four hours of my asking for this type of backup. Similar experiences are so comforting.

Prayer and declaration: Lord, thank You for allowing us to have some control over our spirit man. Help us to be aware of the times when the deep (spirit) in someone else is calling out to our deep (spirit man) and leaving us something of value to carry with us throughout our lifetime.

I now decree and declare that I am in tune with my spirit man and the things God is preparing me for in the days ahead through this heavenly line of communication. I am aware of many more opportunities to pray, intercede and prepare for the things that God, through my spirit, is speaking to me. I declare this authority in Jesus's Name, amen.

Chapter 9

Generational Curses In The Church Family

John 16:13 Amplified Bible (AMP)
13 But when He, the Spirit of Truth, comes, He will guide you
into all the truth [full and complete truth]. For He will not
speak on His own initiative, but He will speak whatever He
hears [from the Father—the message regarding the Son], and
He will disclose to you what is to come [in the future].

Let's begin this chapter by first establishing what a generational curse entails. A generational curse is a bondage or sin passed down from generation to generation. Good examples would be depression, alcoholism, abandonment, victimization, etc. Anything that can put you in bondage to a behavior or sin can be passed down to you.

If you walk in the same behavior that your parents walked in, you will most likely, pass it down to your children. Many in the church believe that these things are not curses at all. They believe that people are stuck with these maladies and sins because these negatives are knit into the genetic makeup which is solely passed through the genes. Genes get turned on and off every day by thoughts and intertwined beliefs and feelings. Operating in generational sin will alter genetic chemistry. Science can back that up and so does the Bible. Numbers 14:18 is just one Scriptural example of how a generational curse works:

Numbers 14:18 Amplified Bible (AMP)
18 'The Lord is slow to anger, and abundant in lovingkindness,
forgiving wickedness, and transgression; but He will by no means

> *clear the guilty, visiting (avenging) the wickedness and guilt of the*
> *fathers on the children, to the third and fourth generations [that*
> *is, calling the children to account for the sins of their fathers].'*

We are by no means stuck with these curses! Under Christ, we have His blood and the power and authority He left us to break them ourselves. The key is that WE must break them. God won't just reach down and do it for us. Many people believe that when Christ died for our sins and ascended to the right hand of the Father, we were no longer subject to family curses. They often quote as biblical backup:

> **Jeremiah 31:29-30 Amplified Bible (AMP)**
> **29 "In those days they will not say again, 'The fathers have**
> **eaten sour grapes, And the children's teeth are set on edge.'**

These are usually the same folks who believe they can not be affected by the demonic realm. We must recognize that we are three part beings. As mentioned in prior chapters, we are made up of spirit, soul and physical body. When we accept Christ as our savior, our spirit gets regenerated by the Holy Spirit. We still have a soul realm and a physical body that can be afflicted and affected by demonic influences. If this weren't so, then as soon as we got saved our emotions as well as our physical bodies would instantaneously be perfect. Let me get real right now. I have been working with beautiful, anointed, saved, many baptized in the Holy Spirit saints, who are seriously afflicted in their soul realm (mind, will, and emotions) and their physical bodies when they come into my office. You can argue with me all you like, but until you have been in my shoes and witnessed on a daily basis the level of demonic stuff leaving people who love the Lord like I do, your argument holds no weight with me. Usually, the people who debate have not personally gone through the process themselves. I have witnessed demonic forces leave people. Many in my office have felt familiar spirits leave their side after praying the generational prayer for each side of their family line. So let's just get past all of these arguments here and now in the body of Christ, shall we? I humbly agree to disagree with the naysayers.

Now let's look at curses attached to the church body. A church body is a living organism. It is a family and just like generational curses can plague a blood family, so also they can affect a church family. Many churches seem to be plagued with the same types of issues among their congregation decade after decade.

Meditating on your own church family will highlight what needs prayer. This also indicates where we need to learn to change our behavior within the Body of Christ. So what are the main curses that plague church families? God did not leave us to figure this out for ourselves. He left us the answers in the book of Revelation which Jesus instructed John to write on the island of Patmos.

Jesus Christ spoke directly to the seven churches and told them what they were dealing with which needed correction. I believe that these churches had fallen into a clear pattern of error. They also became religious (a rote, practical, mindless pattern) about some things, yet other things had been so badly neglected or mis-handled, that they eventually became generational curses upon each of these churches and were passed from generation to generation. Jesus' words give us insight into the main issues we need to correct as individual church bodies. I use "WE" because there is nothing new under the sun. And, as you read the letters to the seven churches in Revelation, you can see that our modern day churches are still being plagued by the same, exact issues.

Let's take a look at the seven churches and discover what may be plaguing your own church families. Please know that this information is not to fuel your fire and have you running in to your pastor to speak condemning words concerning what we believe may be a curse in our church bodies. The pastors probably are already aware (especially if they have an open door policy with church members) of the situation. As mature believers in Christ, we are called to pray when we discover something which needs to be handled. We are also called to examine ourselves and do everything in our power to make sure that we are not part of the problem. It is not until the Lord specifically instructs us to speak that we do so. Even then, seek further confirmation, perhaps even multiple confirmations, before speaking up about a problem such as this that involves an entire church family. The key is if we are aware of it, we can be one person who is standing in the gap for the church body and interceding in prayer.

It is speculated that the seven churches referred to in Revelation were founded around the time that Paul made his three missionary journeys and yet they were not all founded by Paul. We will examine each of the seven churches individually according to what Jesus Christ Himself spoke to them. The church in Ephesus is first:

Revelation 2:1-7 Amplified Bible (AMP)
Message to Ephesus
"To the angel (divine messenger) of the church in [a]Ephesus write:
"These are the words of the One who holds [firmly] the
seven stars [which are the angels or messengers of the seven
churches] in His right hand, the One who walks among
the seven golden lampstands (the seven churches):
2 'I know [b]your deeds and your toil, and your patient endurance,
and that you cannot tolerate those who are evil, and have tested
and critically appraised those who call themselves apostles (special
messengers, personally chosen representatives, of Christ), and [in
fact] are not, and have found them to be liars and impostors; 3 and
[I know that] you [who believe] are enduring patiently and are

*bearing up for My name's sake, and that you have not grown weary
[of being faithful to the truth]. 4 But I have this [charge] against
you, that you have left your first love [you have lost the depth of
love that you first had for Me]. 5 So remember the heights from
which you have fallen, and repent [change your inner self—your
old way of thinking, your sinful behavior—seek God's will] and do
the works you did at first [when you first knew Me]; otherwise, I
will visit you and remove your lampstand (the church, its impact)
from its place—unless you repent. 6 Yet you have this [to your
credit], that you hate the works and corrupt teachings of the [c]
Nicolaitans [that mislead and delude the people], which I also
hate. 7 He who has an ear, let him hear and heed what the Spirit
says to the churches. To him who [d]overcomes [the world through
believing that Jesus is the Son of God], I will grant [the privilege] to
eat [the fruit] from the tree of life, which is in the Paradise of God.'*

Ephesus seems to be dealing with evil men and false apostles. They appear to have a zero tolerance policy for imposters and know how to perform a thorough investigation in order to expose the false and protect those who have a true apostolic calling on their lives. They also appear to possess much perseverance and endurance. Their doctrine is sound. The Lord is pleased by this. What Jesus is grieved over is that they have fallen away from their first love. They have productivity but they have lost their passion and love for Him. Perhaps good works have gotten in the way of their original love for what Christ did for them on the cross. They have made service a priority over spending time to reconnect with Jesus. I believe He is telling them to get back to putting Him first, to being in love with HIm.

I also sense that He could be referring to the prodigals who have once given their hearts to Jesus but then walked away for the things of this world. The name Ephesus has two possible meanings: "desirable" and "permitted". Perhaps the prodigals have gone after the good works of the world and come into agreement with what is desirable and permitted in the land. If this is the case, perhaps a great and powerful prayer would be for the prodigals to return to their first love according to Revelation 2:4. If you are experiencing the heartbreak of having a child/children or grandchildren who are prodigals, I want to give you a key to praying for them. The Lord gave me this key a few years ago when I was deep in worship. He showed me that once your children are adults, your prayers no longer hold as much spiritual weight over their lives as they once had when they were under your tutelage. The way to gain that back is to ask them if they mind if you still cover them spiritually in your prayers. If they give you a verbal "yes", then your prayers will avail more than if you don't have their verbal permission. When

God gave me this key, I was deep in prayer for a young man during a tough time. He was not a prodigal but was struggling with some things that seemed as though they would never break off of his life. As his parents received this key and asked his permission to continue to cover him spiritually as an adult, he gave them his verbal "yes". In exactly forty days from that yes, they saw a major breakthrough for him that they had all been waiting for for quite a few years!

As we continue to look at Ephesus, we see that Jesus also addresses His deep hate for the deeds of the Nicolaitans. Their doctrine is of devils. The Nicolaitans have no problem throwing in occult activities together with their Christianity. The Nicolaitans have deep paganistic roots (generational witchcraft). Jesus ends His message to Ephesus by crediting them with not accepting these corrupt practices.

I see their generational curse is religion which is tied to perfectionism and striving. Good works and the checklist are not more important than time with the Father, Son, and Holy Spirit. They must confess and repent (turn away from) and begin to daily seek the Lord's will regarding their endeavors, their time, talent, and resources. We can also recognize that the generational curses of religion and legalism are the very things that have caused so many prodigals to leave the church to begin with. Religion drives young people away from the church because they are unable to see the love with which the members had first embraced their Savior. I believe, as more churches abandon religion and walk in the love of Christ, more prodigals will be drawn back.

The next church mentioned is the church in Smyrna.

Revelation 2:8-11 Amplified Bible (AMP)

8 "And to the angel (divine messenger) of the church in [a]Smyrna write: "These are the words of the First and the Last [absolute Deity, the Son of God] who died and came to life [again]: 9 'I know your suffering and your poverty (but you are rich), and how you are blasphemed and slandered by those who say they are Jews and are not, but are a synagogue of Satan [they are Jews only by blood, and do not believe and truly honor the God whom they claim to worship]. 10 Fear nothing that you are about to suffer. Be aware that the devil is about to throw some of you into prison, that you may be tested [in your faith], and for ten days you will have tribulation. Be faithful to the point of death [if you must die for your faith], and I will give you the crown [consisting] of life. 11 He who has an ear, let him hear and heed what the Spirit says to the churches. He who overcomes [the world through believing that Jesus is the Son of God] will not be hurt by the second death ([b]the lake of fire).

First, the Greek translation for Smyrna is "myrrh". Myrrh is often remembered as one of the three gifts that the Magi gave to Jesus after He was born. When it is crushed, it is utilized to preserve things including dead bodies.

It's quite apparent through what our Lord Jesus spoke to Smyrna, that they were about to experience a crushing that was beyond their expectations. I don't see anything here that involves generational curses other than the possibility of fear. Jesus is instructing them to fear nothing. The Greek word for fear in this verse is "phobeo" which is the root of our word "phobia". Phobeo means "to frighten, to be alarmed; to be sore afraid, or fear exceedingly or to reverence". Fear is one of the main curses that seems to travel in family lines. We may be asking ourselves at this point if you think you would be afraid if you were the one being told to persevere unto death. Most of us believe we would feel terrified if faced with martyrdom!

I remember a time in recent years when the Islamic extremest group Isis rounded up twenty-one Coptic Christians on a Libyan beachfront and executed them. It was a horrific scene and it struck fear into the hearts of many believers all over the world. I must admit I wrestled for weeks after that heartbreaking event. I asked God over and over if I had what it takes to be tested and tried to the point of death for my faith in Christ. I prayed about this for weeks. One day my answer came by way of an article which featured some interviews of the families of those brave, martyred men. The families shared that the grief of the loss was awful; yet, they felt honored to be among those who had been born for such a time as this to be a sign and a witness to the world for Christ. They spoke of how they believed that those men were anointed and prepared by God Himself to stand up under that trial and to not renounce their faith in Jesus Christ. I realized at that moment that if one has been hand-picked (destined) to suffer any type of persecution, even unto martyrdom, that God is certainly going to equip the person to handle the pressure. The Holy Spirit always gives the grace to accomplish any task He assigns!

2 Corinthians 12:9
but He has said to me, "My grace is sufficient for you [My lovingkindness and My mercy are more than enough—always available—regardless of the situation]; for [My] power is being perfected [and is completed and shows itself most effectively] in [your] weakness." Therefore, I will all the more gladly boast in my weaknesses, so that the power of Christ [may completely enfold me and] may dwell in me.

Getting back to the curses in Smyrna's line, the only possibility other than fear that I see here may be poverty. Although they may have been poor due to the persecution of their faith, even in their poverty, the Lord reminded them that they were rich. He was referring to the eternal crown of life each of them would receive which could not be taken away.

We must remember they were being persecuted by the synagogue of Satan which could symbolize any sect of believers or non-believers who are not acknowledging Jesus as the true Messiah. They were being encouraged to endure persecution for their faith, even unto death. I believe that this applies to each and every true church of Jesus Christ that is preaching the gospel in purity. We must stay on the path of the Way and not be deceived by erroneous ways to God or to peace. Perhaps this warning as well as the encouraging word were necessary in order to ward off any open door which could result in cursing this church's future generations because of their compromise. Perhaps without the warning, they would have begun to add or take away from the pure preaching of the Word.

Revelation 22:18 Amplified Bible (AMP)
18 I testify and warn everyone who hears the words of the prophecy
of this book [its predictions, consolations, and admonitions]: if
anyone adds [anything] to them, God will add to him the plagues
(afflictions, calamities) which are written in this book;

I am sure you are all aware of some churches which have compromised by including all forms of religion. I am thinking of one that embraces each religion including satanism and has no problem exhibiting satanic symbols on their bumper stickers and letterheads while at the same time it communicates the message for us all to peacefully coexist. God was very clear that we are to HATE the things which He hates. He hates the works of the enemy. Of course, we all know that we are to love everyone. We are to hate what sin produces and hate the demonic realm, not people. God loves everyone. I believe this letter to the church of Smyrna is a firm warning to all of us that, as our churches are crushed (perhaps like myrrh) under the weight of the expectation to compromise, that we must remain steadfast and not compromise under the crushing or we too could become synagogues of Satan.

Next is the church of Pergamum

Revelation 2:12-17 Amplified Bible (AMP)
12 "And to the angel (divine messenger) of the church in [a]
Pergamum write: "These are the words of Him who has and wields
the sharp two-edged sword [in judgment]: 13 'I know where you
dwell, [a place] where Satan sits enthroned. Yet you are holding
fast to My name, and you did not deny [b]My faith even in the
days of [c]Antipas, My witness, My faithful one, who was killed

(martyred) among you, where Satan dwells. 14 But I have a few things against you, because you have there some [among you] who are holding to the [corrupt] teaching of Balaam, who taught [d] Balak to put a stumbling block before the sons of Israel, [enticing them] to eat things that had been sacrificed to idols and to commit [acts of sexual] [e]immorality. 15 You also have some who in the same way are holding to the teaching of the [f]Nicolaitans. 16 Therefore repent [change your inner self—your old way of thinking, your sinful behavior—seek God's will]; or else I am coming to you quickly, and I will make war and fight against them with the sword of My mouth [in judgment]. 17 He who has an ear, let him hear and heed what the Spirit says to the churches. To him who overcomes [the world through believing that Jesus is the Son of God], to him I will give [the privilege of eating] some of the [g]hidden manna, and I will give him a [h]white stone with a new name engraved on the stone which no one knows except the one who receives it.'

God has clearly commended the people of the church in Pergamum for holding fast and not denying His Name even when Antipas was martyred. Antipas was a pastor or leader of the church at Pergamum who was killed for his faithfulness. Idolatry and immorality had conquered and mastered the people in this town and the Lord was calling out this church for having some in the church who were holding fast to idolatry. Also, it appears as though they had some who were still engaging in sexual immorality and eating food sacrificed to idols. What does that look like in modern day life? Engaging in sexual immorality would seem clear; yet, maybe it's really not so obvious. We must include adultery, fornication, incest, rape, all forms of molestation as well as pornography, homosexuality, and engaging in prostitution and human trafficking. Let's not forget lusting after other men and women in our hearts. They needed to break the generational ties of idolatry, sexual immorality, occult practices, and all witchcraft. They also needed to renounce ties with their pageanistic roots (Nicolaitans, Balaam, and Balak).

I love how the Lord wrote to them with encouragement that He will come to fight with the sword of His mouth (judgement) against these things. It is their job to confess, repent, and change the way they think so they can be free. Then His sword will come and rightly divide between their soul and spirit and kick the enemy out. I also see here how much more effective they would have been in witnessing in that corrupt city when they were purified and unable to be swayed by co-mingling the ways of the world with their Christianity. This message applies to the modern churches now more than ever. Many have embraced and co-mingled new age practices into their Christianity and called it holy. Many are completely deceived that they are doing anything against God's

Word and will. We need to rely on the Holy Spirit to reveal what we need to remove from our practices and traditions which doesn't line up with the Kingdom. Has your church family or denomination embraced the practices of the world and now accepts and calls them holy?

2 Corinthians 6:17-18 Amplified Bible (AMP)
17"So come out from among unbelievers and be separate,"
says the Lord, "And do not touch what is unclean;
And I will graciously receive you and welcome you [with favor],
18And I will be a Father to you, And you will be My
sons and daughters," Says the Lord Almighty.
Pray for their spiritual eyes to be opened and come out from
there and separate (leave the church) only if the Lord asks
you to do so. If not, stay and intercede on their behalf.

Next, we see the church of Thyatira.

Revelation 2:18-29 Amplified Bible (AMP)
Message to Thyatira
18 "And to the angel (divine messenger) of the church in [a]Thyatira
write: "These are the words of the Son of God, who has eyes [that
flash] like a flame of fire [in righteous judgment], and whose feet
are like burnished [white-hot] bronze: 19 'I know your deeds, your
love and faith and service, and patient endurance, and that your
last deeds are more numerous and greater than the first. 20 But I
have this [charge] against you, that you tolerate the woman Jezebel,
who calls herself a prophetess [claiming to be inspired], and she
teaches and misleads My bond-servants so that they commit [acts
of sexual] immorality and eat food sacrificed to idols. 21 I gave
her time to repent [to change her inner self and her sinful way of
thinking], but she has no desire to repent of her immorality and
refuses to do so. 22 [b]Listen carefully, I will throw her on a bed of
sickness, and those who commit adultery with her [I will bring] into
great anguish, unless they repent of her deeds. 23 And I will kill
her children (followers) with [c]pestilence [thoroughly annihilating
them], and all the churches will know [without any doubt] that
I am He who searches the [d]minds and hearts [the innermost
thoughts, purposes]; and I will give to each one of you [a reward or
punishment] according to your deeds. 24 But to the rest of you in

> *Thyatira, who do not hold this teaching, who have not explored and known the [e]depths of Satan, as they call them—I place no other burden on you, 25 except to hold tightly to what you have until I come. 26 And he who overcomes [the world through believing that Jesus is the Son of God] and he who keeps My deeds [doing things that please Me] until the [very] end, to him I will give authority and power over the nations; 27 and he shall shepherd and rule them with a rod of iron, as the earthen pots are broken in pieces, as I also have received authority [and power to rule them] from My Father; 28 and I will give him the [f]Morning Star. 29 He who has an ear, let him hear and heed what the Spirit says to the churches.'*

This is the longest letter of the seven churches. I love Jesus' exhortation to the church in Thyatira about their love and faith and how much they have endured with people and have strived to be numerous in good deeds, giving grace to all people. Perhaps this warning shows that they have extended too much grace to the point of placating and over-tolerating people who carry Jezebel (can be male or female) tendencies. It is vital that we take a look at the fourteen main characteristics that define the Jezebel spirit. I have chosen to share the late, great, John Paul Jackson's list as a reference. The man was what I consider an expert in his field:

14 Characteristics of the Jezebel spirit
by John Paul Jackson

Here are some of the characteristics that accompany the work of the Jezebel spirit. Please keep in mind that a person heavily influenced by this demonic spirit may do many of the following, at one time or another, although not necessarily in the order described. Furthermore, a single characteristic does not indicate that someone has a "full -blown" Jezebel spirit. It may simply mean that the person is still spiritually and emotionally immature. When a combination of several of the fourteen characteristics exists, however, there is a strong indication that an individual is influenced by a Jezebel spirit. Also, remember that one characteristic may be clearly noticeable, but other traits may be hidden and yet profound. A prolonged manifestation of any of these traits warrants a closer look at the individual and the situation.

1. While it's almost unrecognizable at first, such individuals are threatened by a prophetic leader who is the main target of concern. Although such people will seem to have prophetic gifts, their aim is to actually control those who move in the prophetic realm.

2. To increase their favor, such individuals often zero in on a pastor and church staff, and then seek to find the weakest link in order to subdue them. Their eventual goal is to run the church.

3. Seeking to gain popular and pastoral endorsement, such individuals will form strategic affiliations with people who are perceived by others to be spiritual or influential with others.

4. To appear spiritual, such individuals will seek recognition by manipulating situations to gain an advantage. Such individuals often conjure up dreams and visions from their imaginations, or they borrow them from others.

5. When these individuals receive initial recognition, they often respond with false humility. However, this trait is short-lived.

6. When confronted, these individuals will become defensive. They will justify their actions with phrases like, "I'm just following God" or "God told me to do this."

7. These individuals will often allege having great spiritual insight into church government and affairs, but they will not appeal to proper authority Rather they first appeal to others. Often their opinion becomes the "last word" on matters, thereby elevating their thoughts above the pastor's.

8. Having impure motives, these individuals will seek out others, desiring to have "disciples," needing constant affirmation from their followers.

9. Desiring to avoid accountability, these individuals prefer to pray for people in isolated situations in a corner or in another room. Thus, innuendos and false "prophetic" words cannot be easily challenged.

10. Eager to gain control, these people will gather others and seek to teach them. While the teachings may begin correctly, "doctrine" is often established that is not supported by the Word of God.

11. Deceiving others by soulish prophecy or by giving words that someone wants to hear, these individuals seek to gain credibility. They prophesy half-truth or little known facts, as though they were from God. Such individuals may also take advantage of someone else's poor memory by twisting their previous prophecies to make it seem as if their words have come to pass.

12. Although the "laying on of hands" is biblical, these individuals like to impart a higher level in the spirit or break down walls that have held someone back by the "laying on of hands." However, their touch is actually a curse. Instead of a holy blessing, an evil spirit may be imparted.

13. Masking poor self-esteem with spiritual pride, these individuals want to be seen as the most spiritual ones in the church. They may be the first to cry, wail, or mourn claiming a burden from God. However, they are no different from the Pharisees who announced their gifts in order to be seen by men.

14. Usually, such an individual's family life is shaky. These individuals may be single or married. If married, their spouse is usually weak spiritually, unsaved, or miserable. They begin to dominate and control everyone in the family.

The church in Thyatira appears as though they have allowed too much leeway when these types of people pave the way for immorality and idolatry as well as discord in their own lives, and also lead others astray. The warnings here are severe for Jezebel's children (their followers). I believe the reason why is because no matter how much these people are given allowance to repent, they refuse to do so. That is a clear indication of how you will know them by their fruit. They go back to performing the same unholy acts regardless of how many times they have been corrected. it is not fully implicated what kind of sickbed the Lord is referring to. This is not our concern. Your concern as a church member is to stand in the gap and intercede for anyone within your church body who is allowing the Jezebel spirit to intimidate and run roughshod over the congregation. Confess and repent for yourself in this area and learn to stand up to that manipulative spirit. If you are dealing with this in your congregation, then you most likely attract this type of spiritual attachment through others. This may be operating in one or more, or even quite a few congregants. Learn to love the person, but don't tolerate the spirit operating behind them.

The fifth church to be addressed is Sardis

Revelation 3 Amplified Bible (AMP)
Message to Sardis

*3 "To the angel (divine messenger) of the church in [a]Sardis write:
"These are the words of Him who has [b]the seven Spirits of
God and the seven stars: 'I know your deeds; you have a name
(reputation) that you are alive, but [in reality] you are dead. 2
Wake up, and strengthen and reaffirm what remains [of your
faithful commitment to Me], which is about to die; for I have not
found [any of] your deeds completed in the sight of My God or
meeting His requirements. 3 So remember and take to heart the
lessons you have received and heard. Keep and obey them, and
repent [change your sinful way of thinking, and demonstrate your
repentance with new behavior that proves a conscious decision
to turn away from sin]. So then, if you do not wake up, I will
come like a thief, and you will not know at what hour I will come
to you. 4 But you [still] have a few people in Sardis who have
not soiled their clothes [that is, contaminated their character
and personal integrity with sin]; and they will walk with Me*

[dressed] in white because they are worthy (righteous). 5 He who overcomes [the world through believing that Jesus is the Son of God] will accordingly be dressed in white clothing, and I will never blot out his name from the Book of Life, and I will confess and openly acknowledge his name before My Father and before His angels [saying that he is one of Mine]. 6 He who has an ear, let him hear and heed what the Spirit says to the churches.'

It's so interesting that the church in Sardis had no identified enemy implicated over it. These people were most likely so asleep that they were their own worst enemy. I believe the forces of darkness were stealing territory from this church and they were just allowing it. They were complacent and apathetic, compromising and asleep. I think Jesus gives us a key here as to how they were compromising. He finishes addressing Sardis by telling them that, if they acknowledge Him, He will openly confess them before His Father in heaven. They were most likely falling into line with social pressure. I can't help but think of how the church in the United States stayed silent during the past few decades and allowed so much of God to be taken out of our society. Few were still counted as worthy (clothed in white). Jesus tells them to learn from their lessons in verse three. We too are now learning in recent years from this lesson that began for us I believe in the 1950s & '60s. As the Western church regains its territory, we must remember this lesson! Confess and pray on behalf of your church if it is compromising and allowing societal pressure to steal its voice.

There is also a reference as to their works not being perfected (or completed) in the sight of God. The Greek root word for perfected or completed in this passage means to "consecrate" or "accomplish". To me, this sounds like many contemporary churches who are spiritually sleeping because they will not allow the Holy Spirit to have control. The church can not be alive and operating with fire and power (awake and filled) if the Holy Spirit is not welcomed. I recently heard a powerful statement. I can't recall who said it, but they stated that if a church is operating on Father and Son minus the Holy Spirit, it is operating only at 66.6%. Anytime the number 666 pops up, it should grab our attention. The Lord also warns them to wake up or He will come like a thief when they least expect Him.

If your church does not welcome the presence of the Holy Spirit and allow Him to have control, confess and repent and stand in the gap in prayer. Begin to pray that this generational ignoring of the Holy Spirit and the spirit of religion to be broken in Jesus' Name.

The next church to be addressed is Philadelphia

Message to Philadelphia
7 "And to the angel (divine messenger) of the
church in [c]Philadelphia write:
"These are the words of the Holy One, the True One, He who
has the key [to the house] of David, He who opens and no one
will [be able to] shut, and He who shuts and no one opens:
8 'I know your deeds. See, I have set before you an open door which
no one is able to shut, for you have a little power, and have kept My
word, and have not renounced or denied My name. 9 Take note, I
will make those of the synagogue of Satan, who say that they are
Jews and are not, but lie—I will make them come and bow down
at your feet and make them know [without any doubt] that I have
loved you. 10 Because you have kept the word of My endurance
[My command to persevere], I will keep you [safe] from the hour
of trial, that hour which is about to come on the whole [inhabited]
world, to test those who live on the earth. 11 I am coming quickly.
Hold tight what you have, so that no one will take your crown [by
leading you to renounce the faith]. 12 He who overcomes [the world
through believing that Jesus is the Son of God], I will make him a
[d]pillar in the temple of My God; he will most certainly never be
put out of it, and I will write on him the name of My God, and the
name of the city of My God, the new Jerusalem, which descends out
of heaven from My God, and My [own] new name. 13 He who has an
ear, let him hear and heed what the Spirit says to the churches.'

Even with the little power the church in Philadelphia had, they did not renounce or deny the Name of Jesus when the synagogue of Satan came against them. They endured and this has caused our Lord Jesus to promise them eternal life that no one could take away from them because they understood that He alone is the only door through which salvation comes. It also appears that they are kept from enduring any further testing of their faith.

In other translations, verse seven refers to Jesus as the door. This door means a literal portal in which only Jesus has the key to entry. This signifies that Jesus is the only way to heaven and those who are persecuting anyone for preaching the pure Word will one day bow at their feet.

The only reference to anything that seems negative is that they didn't possess much power. The translation for this word is "dunamis", which means "miraculous power", "mighty work" and "strength". If you see that your church is weak in the demonstration of the supernatural power of God through miracles, signs, and wonders, pray that any religious strongholds of doubt and unbelief, as well as fear of man, be broken in Jesus name. Pray for a strong resolve and an increase in power in order to hold up under pressure when you are pressed to compromise Jesus as Lord, or the pure Word of God.

The final church to be addressed is Laodicea.

Revelation 3:14-22 Amplified Bible (AMP)
Message to Laodicea

14 "To the angel (divine messenger) of the church in [e] Laodicea write: "These are the words of the Amen, the trusted and faithful and true Witness, the [f]Beginning and Origin of God's creation: 15 'I know your deeds, that you are [g]neither cold (invigorating, refreshing) nor hot (healing, therapeutic); I wish that you were [h] cold or hot. 16 So because you are lukewarm (spiritually useless) and neither hot nor cold, I will vomit you out of My mouth [rejecting you with disgust]. 17 Because you say, "I am rich, and have prospered and grown wealthy, and have need of nothing," and you do not know that you are wretched and miserable and poor and blind and naked [without hope and in great need], 18 I counsel you to buy from Me gold that has been heated red hot and refined by fire so that you may become truly rich; and white clothes [representing righteousness] to clothe yourself so that the shame of your nakedness will not be seen, a healing salve to put on your eyes so that you may see. 19 Those whom I [dearly and tenderly] love, I rebuke and discipline [showing them their faults and instructing them]; so be enthusiastic and repent [change your inner self—your old way of thinking, your sinful behavior—seek God's will]. 20 Behold, I stand at the door [of the church] and continually knock. If anyone hears My voice and opens the door, I will come in and eat with him (restore him), and he with Me. 21 He who overcomes [the world through believing that Jesus is the Son of God], I will grant to him [the privilege] to sit beside Me on My throne, as I also overcame and sat down beside My Father on His throne. 22 He who has an ear, let him hear and heed what the Spirit says to the churches."'

The church in Laodicea was self-sufficient financially which made them complacent. According to some commentaries, their works were worthless. The congregation needed, for its own sake, to suffer some persecution in order to destroy its complacency. Persecution tests and strengthens our faith. Jesus states that they need to be refined in the fire in order to become truly rich. The Lord stated that He chastens those whom He loves.

Revelation 3:19 Amplified Bible (AMP)
19 Those whom I [dearly and tenderly] love, I rebuke and
discipline [showing them their faults and instructing them]; so
be enthusiastic and repent [change your inner self—your old
way of thinking, your sinful behavior—seek God's will].

It doesn't sound like the Laodiceans are enduring much if any, persecution. The enemy didn't need to come against them because they weren't a threat to his demonic realm. Being lukewarm is compromise and it's a stronghold. They were settling for a mediocre relationship with God. Being paralyzed and complacent feels easier but, there is no fruit produced. These people needed to be purified and refined in God's fire and thereby come out as pure gold.

This reminds me of one massively huge sect of Christianity that has money and power. There are lots of rituals and much idolatry, but many are not saved therefore are not producing any fruit in their lives.

Jeremiah 17:5
Thus says the Lord, "Cursed is the man who trusts in and relies
on mankind, Making [weak, faulty human] flesh his strength,
And whose mind and heart turn away from the Lord.

Rituals and traditions don't equate to running passionately after the heart of God. If your church is just "playing church" through the use of rituals and idolatry or maybe they are operating in a way that shows they are more interested in looking like the world in hopes of increasing their numbers and filling seats, then pray for the stronghold of lukewarmness to be broken in Jesus' Name. Many individuals are also walking around in a state of apathy and complacency regarding their relationship with Christ. If you feel like this could be you, confess and repent and ask God to help you love Him passionately the way He deserves to be loved.

I thought it would be beautiful to formulate a decree to speak out over all of our churches. The insight that I felt the Lord gave me for this declaration was to combine the issues that the seven churches needed to address and speak correction over them by turning them into a positive, opposite statement. This can be a powerful tool to assist in rooting out the negative spiritual ties existing in any church body. For example, if a church was not enduring patiently to the end, this proclamation states that they ARE enduring with much patience until the end of time. You will see that this prayer combines the seven churches together in order to form one blanket coverage for your church.

I decree and declare that _____(fill in name of your church)

(Ephesus) 'toils with patient endurance, and cannot tolerate those who are evil. The church has tested and critically appraised those who call themselves apostles)and, in fact, are not, and have found them to be liars and impostors. We who believe are enduring patiently and are bearing up for Jesus' sake and have not grown weary of being faithful to the truth. We remember our First Love. Together with Jesus, we hate the works and corrupt teachings of the Nicolaitans (dominating and seducing people to error) that mislead and delude the people.

(Smyrna) We may sometimes suffer but we are rich in Christ. We will fear nothing that we suffer, even being blasphemed and slandered. When we are tested in our faith and experience tribulation, we will be faithful to the point of death and we will receive the crown of life. We will not be hurt by the second death.

(Pergamum) For those of us who dwell, where Satan sits enthroned, we are holding fast to Jesus' Name, and will not deny Him. We do not allow people into the church who put a stumbling block before our sons and daughters, enticing them to eat things that have been sacrificed to idols and to commit [acts of sexual immorality). We repent of our sinful deeds and this gives us the promise of eating the hidden manna and obtaining a white stone in which our new names are engraved.

(Thyatira) Our deeds, our love, and faith, and service are accomplished with patient endurance. Our last deeds are more numerous and greater than our first. We do not tolerate the woman Jezebel who calls herself a prophetess. Our church body repents for committing adultery with her. We will hold on tightly to what we have.

(Sardis) Our church is alive and not dead! We strengthen and affirm our commitment to God. Our deeds are found completed in the sight of God and they meet His requirements. We take to heart the lessons we have received and heard. We keep and obey them. We repent and make a conscious decision to turn away from sin whenever necessary. We have not soiled our clothes that is, contaminated our character and personal integrity with sin and we will walk with Jesus in white because we are worthy (righteous). We will overcome and be acknowledged before the Father. We are awake. We take to heart the lessons we have received and heard.

(Philadelphia) The Lord has set before us an open door that no one is able to shut because we have all the power to defeat the enemy and have kept God's Word. We have not renounced nor denied Jesus. Jesus Himself will make those of the synagogue of Satan who say that

they are Jews and are not, to come and bow down at our feet and cause them to know without any doubt that He loves us. We keep the word of His endurance (His command to persevere), and He keeps us safe from the hour of trial which is about to come on the whole world to test those who live on the earth. We hold tight to what we have so that no one will take our crowns by leading us to renounce the faith. We will overcome the world through believing that Jesus is the Son of God, and we will be pillars in the temple of our God.

(Laodicea) We are on fire for Jesus. We are rich in Him. We buy gold from the Lord that has been heated red hot and refined by fire so that we may become truly rich. Healing salve is put on our eyes so that we may see. Those whom God loves He rebukes and disciplines showing them their faults and instructing them. We are enthusiastic and repent and change our inner self—our old ways of thinking, our sinful behavior and seek God's will. We open the door to Jesus' voice when He knocks. Jesus comes in and eats with us and restores us. We declare all of these things for ourselves, our families, and our church family in Jesus' Name, amen.

I found it fitting to end this book with the roots of our church families as found in the book of Revelation since Revelation is the last book in the Holy Bible. My prayer for you as the reader is that God will anoint you with the wisdom and insight to continue to discover concealed roots in your own life, as well as your family's, lives. May you receive the wisdom to pull those roots out by the Spirit of God and in Jesus' name, Amen.

Bibliography

John Paul Jackson - streamsministries.com

owlcation.com

biblegateway.com

dictionary.com

Printed in the United States
By Bookmasters